Ambedkar and Buddhism

Dr B. R. Ambedkar

Ambedkar and Buddhism
Sangharakshita

Windhorse Publications

Ambedkar and Buddhism

Windhorse Publications
136 Renfield Street
Glasgow
G2 3AU

Printed by Richard Clay
(The Chaucer Press) Ltd.,
Bungay, Suffolk

Cover illustration by Dharmacharis Dhammarati and Paramabodhi
Frontispiece by Dharmachari Aloka
ISBN 0 904766 28 4

First edition 1986
Reprinted 1989

Cataloguing-in-Publication data available

Contents

For thirty years, Sangharakshita has been playing a crucial part in the spread of Buddhism throughout the modern world. He is the head of the Western Buddhist Order (Trailokya Bauddha Mahasangha), and is actively engaged in the development of what is now an international Buddhist movement with centres in twelve countries worldwide. When not visiting centres, he is based at a community in Norfolk. His writings are available in ten languages.

Also by Sangharakshita:

Messengers from Tibet and Other Poems

A Survey of Buddhism

Flame in Darkness

The Enchanted Heart

The Three Jewels

The Essence of Zen

The Thousand-Petalled Lotus

Human Enlightenment

The Religion of Art

The Ten Pillars of Buddhism

The Eternal Legacy

Travel Letters

Alternative Traditions

Conquering New Worlds

Crossing the Stream

The History of My Going For Refuge

The Meaning of Orthodoxy in Buddhism

Mind—Reactive and Creative

Aspects of Buddhist Morality

Buddhism and Blasphemy

Buddhism, World Peace, and Nuclear War

The Bodhisattva: Evolution and Self-Transcendence

The Glory of the Literary World

Going For Refuge

The Caves of Bhaja

*No volcano bursting up through peaceful pastures is
a greater revolution than this;*
*No vast mountain chain thrown from ocean depths
to form the primitive streak of a new continent looks further
down the future;*
*For this lava springing out of the very heart of
Man;*
*This is the upheaval of heaven-kissing summits whose
streams shall feed the farthest generations,*
This is the draft and outline of a new creature,
*The forming of the wings of Man beneath the outer
husk—*
*The outspread pinions of Equality, whereon arising he
shall at last lift himself over the Earth and launch forth
to sail through Heaven.*

Edward Carpenter (1844—1929) 'Towards Democracy'

Preface

There are at present 100,000,000 Untouchables in India, the vast majority of whom are underprivileged in every sense of the term. Each year between four and five hundred of them are murdered by their Caste Hindu compatriots, while thousands more are beaten, raped, and tortured and their homes looted and burned. An incalculable number of them are not only subject to social, economic, and religious discrimination but daily suffer personal harassment and humiliation.

In the course of the last thousand or so years saints and reformers have sought to ameliorate the lot of the Untouchables—none of them with any great success. The latest and most heroic of these attempts was made by Dr Bhimrao Ramji Ambedkar, himself an Untouchable by birth, who came to the conclusion that there was no salvation for the Untouchables within Hinduism and that they would have to change their religion. In October 1956 he and half a million of his followers therefore became Buddhists, thus bringing about the renaissance of Buddhism in India and initiating a religious and social revolution of major significance.

Though the sufferings of the Jews in Nazi Germany and of the blacks in white supremacist South Africa are well known and widely discussed, the no less horrifying sufferings of the Untouchables at the hands of the Caste Hindus, as well as Ambedkar's heroic efforts to emancipate his people from their age-old slavery, have remained virtually unknown outside India. Thirty years after his death, the West has yet to see a biography of the great untouchable leader, while there is still no sign of a book-length study of the movement of mass conversion to Buddhism which he inaugurated.

The present work cannot be considered as remedying these deficiencies, but only as taking a small step in that direction. In the following pages I have given a brief account of Ambedkar's career, described why and how he became a Buddhist, and explained what Buddhism meant to him. Since the work is of a popular rather than a scholarly nature Sanskrit and Pali words have in most cases not been given their diacritical marks and there has been no attempt to secure uniformity in the spelling of these words as between my own text and the various quotations from Ambedkar's writings.

I would like to thank Dharmacharis Lokamitra, Dharmarakshita, and Vimalakirti (all of Poona) for supplying me with books that were either out of print or unobtainable in England, Elaine Murray for typing the manuscript, Dharmachari Aloka for designing the cover and drawing the frontispiece, and Dharmachari Shantavira for editing the manuscript and seeing the work through the press.

Sangharakshita

1

The Significance of Ambedkar

In the grounds of the parliament building in Delhi stands a statue of a stout, elderly man clad in a business suit and wearing spectacles. The statue is about fifteen feet high, and stands with right foot slightly advanced on the square top of a pedestal of much the same height. Underneath the left arm of the statue is a large book, while its right arm is outstretched practically to its full extent, index finger pointing in the direction of the parliament building. The statue represents Bhimrao Ramji Ambedkar, Law Minister in the Government of India from 1947 to 1951; the book underneath his arm is the Indian Constitution, and his finger points to the parliament building because it was there that in 1948 he presented his draft Constitution to the Constituent Assembly, there that it was accepted a year later, and there that the legislation based on its provisions has ever since been passed.

Bhimrao Ramji Ambedkar was one of the most remarkable men of his time, and the story of his life is the story of how exceptional talent and outstanding force of character succeeded in overcoming some of the most formidable obstacles that an unjust and oppressive society has ever placed in the way of the individual. Born in Mhow in central India in 1891, he was the fourteenth child of parents who belonged to the very lowest stratum of Hindu society. According to orthodox Hindu tradition, he was not entitled to receive education or to acquire property, he could engage only in the most menial and degrading work, and he could not come into physical contact with members of the higher castes. In short, Bhimrao Ramji Ambedkar was born an outcaste or Untouchable. He was expected to wear cast-off clothes, to eat the leavings of his higher caste masters, to be humble and obedient, and to accept his lot as the well-deserved punishment for sins committed in a former existence.

Fortunately for him, however, his father had served in the Indian Army and there acquired a certain amount of formal education in both Marathi and English. This enabled him to teach his children, especially Bhimrao Ramji, and to encourage them in their own pursuit of knowledge. In 1908 the young Ambedkar passed the matriculation examination of Bombay University, and so uncommon was such an achievement on the part of an Untouchable boy that the event was celebrated with a public meeting. Four years later he graduated from the same university with Politics and Economics as subjects and soon afterwards entered the service of the Baroda State, the ruler of which had awarded him a scholarship. At this point his father died (his mother had died when he was five) and four months later the bereaved son left India to continue his studies at Columbia University (USA) on a further scholarship from the same liberal-minded ruler. Though he had climbed higher up the ladder of academic achievement than any other Untouchable, Ambedkar was far from being satisfied. Convinced as he was that knowledge is power, he knew that without that power in full measure he had little hope of breaking the bonds that kept millions of Untouchables in a state of virtual slavery—and how strong those bonds were his own bitter personal experience had already taught him.

From 1913 to 1917, and again from 1920 to 1923, Ambedkar was in the West, and when at the age of thirty-two he finally returned to the country of his birth it was as one of the most highly qualified men in public life. During his three years at Columbia University he studied Economics, Sociology, History,

Philosophy, Anthropology, and Politics, and was awarded a Ph.D. for the thesis which he eventually published in book form as *The Evolution of Provincial Finance in British India.* His first published work, however, was a paper on 'Castes in India: Their Mechanism, Genesis and Development' which he had originally read at an Anthropology seminar conducted by one of his professors. After completing his studies in America, Ambedkar left New York for London, where he was admitted to the London School of Economics and Political Science and to Gray's Inn. A year later his scholarship came to an end and it was only in 1920 that, having taught in a Bombay college and started a Marathi weekly called *Mooknayak* or 'Leader of the Dumb', he was able to return to London and resume his studies there. In the course of the next three years he completed his thesis on *The Problem of the Rupee,* for which the University of London awarded him a D.Sc., and was called to the Bar. Before leaving England he spent three months in Germany, where he engaged in further studies in Economics at the University of Bonn.

Thus the man who returned to India in April 1923 to continue his fight on behalf of the Untouchables and, indeed, all the Depressed Classes, was uniquely well equipped for the task, and from this time onwards it becomes increasingly difficult to separate the biography of Bhimrao Ramji Ambedkar from the history of modern India. During his three year absence in London the Indian political scene had changed dramatically. The demand for independence from Britain had grown louder than ever: Mahatma Gandhi had started advocating a policy of non-cooperation with the Government and only a year before Ambedkar's return had launched the first of his campaigns for mass civil disobedience. But though Ambedkar was a staunch patriot, and though initially he was of the opinion that only political independence would bring social equality within the reach of the Depressed Classes, he was emphatic that if—as Gandhi and the Congress Party maintained—no country was good enough to rule over another it was equally true that no class was good enough to rule over another class. Certainly the Caste Hindus were not good enough to lord it over the Depressed Classes, and while Ambedkar remained sharply critical of British

5

rule it was to the removal of the social, economic, educational, and legal disabilities of the Depressed Classes that he devoted the major part of his energies. As early as 1920 he had realized, however, that the interests of the Depressed Classes would have to be safeguarded by means of separate electorates, at least for a period, and it was his increasing insistence on this point that eventually brought him into open conflict with Mahatma Gandhi and the Congress Party, as well as with practically the whole of orthodox Hindu India.

This conflict did not come to a head until 1932. In the meantime Ambedkar established himself in Bombay, built up his legal practice, taught in college, gave evidence before various official bodies, started a newspaper, and was nominated to the Bombay Legislative Council, in whose proceedings he at once took a leading part. He also attended the three Round Table Conferences that were held in London to enable representatives of the various Indian communities and the three British political parties to consider proposals for the future constitution of India. One of his most significant achievements during the years immediately following his return to India in 1923 was the formation of the Bahishkrit Hitakarini Sabha or Depressed Classes Welfare Association, the objects of which were to promote the spread of education and culture among the Depressed Classes, to improve their economic condition, and to represent their grievances.

These grievances were serious enough. Untouchables were not allowed to enter Hindu temples, they could not draw water from public tanks or wells, they were denied admittance to schools, and prevented from moving about freely in public places—and so on. Between 1927 and 1932 Ambedkar therefore led his followers in a series of non-violent campaigns to assert the right of the Untouchables to enter Hindu places of worship and to draw water from public tanks and wells. Two of these campaigns were of special importance. These were the campaigns against the exclusion of Untouchables from the Kalaram Temple, Nasik, and from the Chowdar Tank, Mahad, both of which involved tens of thousands of Untouchable satyagrahis or 'passive resisters', provoked a violently hostile reaction from the Caste Hindus and, in the case of the Chowdar Tank campaign, resulted in a legal as well as a moral victory for the Depressed Classes only after years of litigation. The Chowdar Tank campaign also saw the ceremonial burning of the *Manusmriti* or 'Institutes of Manu', the ancient Hindu law book that bore much of the responsibility for the cruel and degrading treatment that the Untouchables had hitherto suffered at the hands of the Caste Hindus. By committing the much-revered volume to the flames the Depressed Classes were serving notice to the orthodox Hindu community that in future they intended to be treated as human beings.

Unpopular as Ambedkar's activities had already made him with the Caste Hindus, during 1931 and 1932 he became more unpopular still. In his own words, he became the most hated man in India—hated, that is, by the Caste Hindus and by the Congress Party, which they dominated. The cause of the trouble was Ambedkar's continued insistence on the necessity of separate electorates for the Depressed Classes. Mahatma Gandhi and the Congress Party were opposed to separate electorates for the Depressed Classes (though not for the Muslims, Sikhs, Christians, and Europeans), and Ambedkar and Gandhi had clashed on the subject at the Second Round Table Conference, when the Mahatma went so far as to challenge the right of Ambedkar to represent the Untouchables. Ambedkar's arguments did, however, convince the British Government, and when Ramsay MacDonald published his Communal Award the following year the Depressed Classes were given the separate electorates for which they had asked. Gandhi's response was to go on a fast to the death for the abolition of separate electorates for the Depressed Classes. Since he was the acknowledged leader of the independence movement his action created consternation throughout India. Ambedkar was reviled as a traitor and threats were made against his life. But though unmoved by the pressure that was brought to bear on him Ambedkar was not unwilling to negotiate and eventually agreed to exchange separate electorates for joint electorates and a greatly increased number of reserved seats. This agreement was embodied in a document that became known as the Poona Pact, the signing of which by Ambedkar marked his emergence as the undisputed leader of the Depressed Classes.

In the mood of relief that swept the country when the weak and ailing Mahatma ended his fast there was even a little sympathy to spare for the wretched Untouchables, but it did not last long, and soon Ambedkar was as much hated as ever. Partly as a result of the opposition he had encountered over the question of separate electorates, partly because of the continued exclusion of Untouchables from Hindu temples, Ambedkar now began to think that the Caste Hindus were not going to mend their ways. He therefore changed his tactics—though not his strategy—and started exhorting his followers to concentrate on raising their standard of living and gaining political power. He also began to think that there was no future for the Untouchables within Hinduism and that they should change their religion. These thoughts found dramatic expression at the 1935 Depressed Classes Conference, when he made his famous declaration that though he had been born a Hindu he did not intend to die one— a declaration that sent shock waves through Hindu India. In the same year Ambedkar was appointed principal of the Government Law College, Bombay, built a house for himself and his books, and lost his wife Ramabai. They had been married in 1908, when he was sixteen and she was nine and she had borne him five children, of whom only one survived. Though the demands of public life had left him with little time for his own domestic affairs, Ambedkar was deeply attached to the gentle and self-effacing woman and mourned her bitterly.

When he had recovered from his grief he plunged back into his customary activities and soon was busier than ever. In the course of the next few years he founded the Independent Labour Party, took part in the provincial elections that were held under the Government of India Act, 1935, was elected to the Bombay Legislative Assembly, pressed for the abolition of agricultural serfdom, defended the right of industrial workers to strike, advocated the promotion of birth control, and addressed meetings and conferences all over the Bombay Presidency. In 1939 World War II broke out in Europe and the fact that Britain was locked in a life-and-death struggle with Nazi Germany soon had its effect on the political situation in India. According to Gandhi and the Congress Party, Britain's difficulty was India's opportunity, and from 1940 they adopted a policy of non-cooperation with the Government war effort. Ambedkar did not agree with this attitude. Not only was he not a pacifist but he regarded Nazi ideology as a direct threat to the liberties of the Indian people. He therefore exhorted them to help defeat Nazism by supporting the Government, and himself encouraged the Untouchables to join the Indian Army. In 1941 he was appointed to the Defence Advisory Committee and in the following year joined the Viceroy's Executive Council as Labour Member, a post he occupied for the next four years. During the same period he transformed the Independent Labour Party into the All-India Scheduled Caste Federation, founded the People's Education Society, and published a number of highly controversial books and pamphlets. Among the latter were *Thoughts on Pakistan, What Congress and Gandhi have Done to the Untouchables,* and *Who Were the Shudras?*

In 1947 India achieved independence and Ambedkar, who had already been elected a member of the Constituent Assembly, was invited by Pandit Nehru, the first prime minister of the country, to join the Cabinet as Minister for Law. A few weeks later the Assembly entrusted the task of framing the Constitution to a Draft Committee, and this committee elected Ambedkar as its chairman. For the next two years he was hard at work on the Draft Constitution, hammering it out article by article and clause by clause practically singlehanded. While he was thus engaged the country was passing through a period of turmoil. Independence had been won only at the cost of partition, partition had led to the wholesale slaughter of Hindus by Muslims and Muslims by Hindus, and at the beginning of 1948 Mahatma Gandhi was assassinated. Besides being deeply concerned about the fate of the Untouchables living in what was now Pakistan Ambedkar had troubles of his own to face. His health had been deteriorating for some time, and now gave him cause for such grave concern that on the day following his fifty-eighth birthday he married a Brahmin woman doctor whom he had met in hospital and who would, he hoped, be able to provide him with the care he needed.

Despite his ill health Ambedkar managed to complete the Draft Constitution by the beginning of 1948 and later that year, when it had been before the country for six months, had the satisfaction of introducing it in the Constituent Assembly. Thereafter he piloted it through its three readings with his usual competence and in November 1949 it was adopted by the Assembly with very few amendments. The new Constitution gave general satisfaction and Ambedkar was warmly congratulated by friend and foe alike. Never had he been so popular. The press hailed him as the Modern Manu, and the irony of the fact that it was an Untouchable who had given Free India its Constitution was widely commented upon. Though he lived for seven more years, it was as the Architect of the Constitution and the Modern Manu that he was destined to pass into official history. When his statue came to be erected outside the parliament building after his death it was therefore as the Modern Manu that he was depicted, holding the Constitution underneath his arm and pointing in the direction of the parliament building. But though by 1948 Ambedkar had achieved so much, and though today he is most widely remembered as the author of the Indian Constitution, his greatest achievement was in fact still to come.

This achievement was an essentially spiritual one, and it came only at the very end of his life, when he had spent several years in the political wilderness after failing to secure the passage of the Hindu Code Bill. The Bill represented a putting into shape by Ambedkar of work accomplished during the previous decade by a number of eminent Hindu lawyers and dealt with such matters as marriage and divorce, adoption, joint family property, women's property, and succession. Though it was a reforming rather than a revolutionary measure, the Bill met with violent opposition both inside and outside the Assembly, and even within the Cabinet. Ambedkar was accused of trying to destroy Hinduism and there were angry exchanges on the Assembly floor between him and his orthodox opponents. In the end the Bill was dropped after only four clauses had been passed and in

September 1951, tired and disgusted, Ambedkar resigned from the Cabinet. In his resignation statement (which he was prevented from making in the Assembly itself) he explained that he had left the Cabinet for five reasons. The second of these was that it was apathetic to the uplift of the Scheduled Castes, the fifth that Pandit Nehru had failed to give adequate support to the Hindu Code Bill.

Ambedkar's resignation from the Cabinet marked the virtual end of his political career. In the general elections of January 1952 he failed to win a seat in the Lok Sabha or House of Representatives, and was equally unsuccessful when he contested a by-election the following year. Towards the end of March 1952 he was, however, elected to the Rajya Sabha or Council of States as one of the seventeen representatives of the State of Bombay, and was soon vigorously attacking the Government. But while he continued to participate in the proceedings of the Rajya Sabha, and was to do so until the end of his life, from now onwards Ambedkar's energies were increasingly devoted to more important things. Ever since the 1935 Depressed Classes Conference, when he had shocked Hindu India with the declaration that though he had been born a Hindu he did not intend to die one, he had been giving earnest consideration to the question of conversion. The longer he thought about it the more he was convinced that there was no future for the Untouchables within Hinduism, that they would have to adopt another religion, and that the best religion for them to adopt was Buddhism. During his years in office it had been hardly possible for him to bring about so momentous a change, but he had lost no opportunity of educating his followers in the issues involved, and it became increasingly apparent in which direction he—and they—were moving. In 1950 he not only praised the Buddha at the expense of Krishna, Christ, and Mohammed but also visited Ceylon at the invitation of the Young Men's Buddhist Association, Colombo, addressed a meeting of the World Fellowship of Buddhists in Kandy, and appealed to the Untouchables of Ceylon to embrace Buddhism. In 1951 he defended the Buddha against the charge that he had been responsible for the downfall of the Indian woman and compiled the *Bauddha Upasana Patha,* a small collection of Buddhist devotional texts. Thus when his resignation from the Cabinet, and his failure to secure election to the Lok Sabha, finally left Ambedkar with the time and energy for his greatest achievement, the ground was already well prepared.

In 1954 he twice visited Burma, the second time in order to attend the third conference of the World Fellowship of Buddhists in Rangoon. In 1955 he founded the Bharatiya Bauddha Mahasabha or Indian Buddhist Society and installed an image of the Buddha in a temple that had been built at Dehu Road, near Poona. Addressing the thousands of Untouchables who had assembled for the occasion, he declared that henceforth he would devote himself to the propagation of Buddhism in India. He also announced that he was writing a book explaining the tenets of Buddhism in simple language for the benefit of the common man. It might take him a year to complete the book, but when it was finished he would embrace Buddhism. The work in question was *The Buddha and His Dhamma,* on which he had been working since November 1951 and which he completed in February 1956. Not long afterwards Ambedkar, true to his word, announced that he would be embracing Buddhism in October of that year. Arrangements were accordingly made for the ceremony to be held in Nagpur, and on 14 October 1956 the Untouchable leader took the Three Refuges and Five Precepts from a Buddhist monk in the traditional manner and then in his turn administered them to the 380,000 men, women, and children who had come to Nagpur in response to his call.[1] After further conversion ceremonies in Nagpur and Chanda Ambedkar returned to Delhi knowing that the Wheel of the Dharma had again been set in motion in India. A few weeks later he travelled to Kathmandu in Nepal for the fourth conference of the World Fellowship of Buddhists and addressed the delegates on 'The Buddha and Karl Marx'. On his way back to Delhi he made two speeches in Benares and visited Kusinara, where the Buddha had died. In Delhi he took part in various Buddhist functions, attended the Rajya Sabha, and completed the last chapter of his book *The Buddha and Karl Marx.* On the evening of 5 December he asked for the Preface and Introduction to

The Buddha and His Dhamma to be brought to his bedside, so that he could work on them during the night, and the following morning he was found dead. It was 6 December, he was 64 years and 7 months old, and he had been a Buddhist for only seven weeks.

But though Bhimrao Ramji Ambedkar had been a Buddhist for only seven weeks, during that period he had probably done more for the promotion of Buddhism than any other Indian since Ashoka. At the time of his death three quarters of a million Untouchables had become Buddhists, and in the months that followed hundreds of thousands more took the same step—despite the uncertainty and confusion that had been created by the sudden loss of their great leader. So much was this the case that when the results of the 1961 census were published it was found that in the course of the previous decade the number of Buddhists in India had risen by a staggering 1,671 per cent and that they now numbered 3,250,227, more than three quarters of whom lived in the State of Maharashtra. This was Ambedkar's last and greatest achievement, so that even though it was as the Architect of the Constitution of Free India and the Modern Manu that he passed into official history and is today most widely remembered, his real significance consists in the fact that it was he who established a revived Indian Buddhism on a firm foundation. It is therefore as the Modern Ashoka that he really deserves to be known, and the statue standing outside the parliament building in Delhi should really depict him holding *The Buddha and His Dhamma* underneath his arm and pointing—not for the benefit of the Untouchables only, but for the benefit of all mankind—in the direction of the Three Jewels.

In order to appreciate the nature of Ambedkar's achievement, and thus the real significance of the man himself, it will however be necessary for us to take a look at the diabolical system from which he sought to deliver the Untouchables, as well as to trace the successive stages of the road by which he—and his followers—travelled from Hinduism to Buddhism. We shall also have to see the way in which Ambedkar discovered his spiritual roots, explore his thoughts on the subject of the Buddha and the future of his religion, survey the historic occasion on which he and 380,000 Untouchables were spiritually reborn, study his posthumously published magnum opus and, finally, see what happened after his death.

But before that, a few personal recollections may not be out of place.

2

Three Meetings

I knew Ambedkar only during the latter part of his life, when he
was in his early sixties and I was in my late twenties and early
thirties. Our three meetings may not have been very important to
him, but they were certainly important to me, and after his death
they were to be of considerable importance for the movement of
conversion to Buddhism which he had inaugurated. In both
background and temperament we were very different, and had it
not been for our common allegiance to Buddhism it is doubtful
if our paths would ever have crossed. I had been born in London
in 1925, two years after Ambedkar had returned to India on the
completion of his studies in the West. At the age of sixteen I read
The Diamond Sutra and *The Sutra of Wei Lang* and thereupon
realized that I was a Buddhist and had, in fact, always been one.
Two years later, World War II having broken out, I was
conscripted into the British Army and posted first to India, then
to Ceylon, and finally to Singapore. At the end of 1946 I left the
army and after spending two years in South India as a
wandering ascetic visited the Buddhist sacred places of north-
east India and was ordained as a shramanera or novice monk.

1949 was spent mainly in Benares, studying Pali and Buddhist Philosophy, and early in 1950 my teacher took me up to Kalimpong, in the foothills of the eastern Himalayas, and told me to stay there and work for the good of Buddhism.

In obedience to these instructions I founded the Young Men's Buddhist Association (Kalimpong) and started publishing a monthly magazine of Himalayan Buddhism called *Stepping-Stones*. Shortly afterwards I wrote to Ambedkar telling him what I had done and received from him a friendly and encouraging reply in the course of which he said, 'Great responsibility lies on the shoulders of the Bhikkhus if this attempt at the revival of Buddhism is to be a success. They must be more active than they have been. They must come out of their shell and be in the front rank of the fighting forces.' His name had been familiar to me since 1949, when I heard it in connection with the controversy that was beginning to rage over the proposed Hindu Code Bill, but it was only after reading his article on 'The Buddha and the Future of His Religion' in the April—May 1950 issue of the *Maha Bodhi*, the monthly journal of the Maha Bodhi Society of India, that I came to understand how deep was his interest in Buddhism and decided to get in touch with him. Towards the end of 1952 I was in Calcutta, writing a Biographical Sketch of Anagarika Dharmapala, the founder of the Maha Bodhi Society of India, for the Society's *Diamond Jubilee Souvenir*, and the successful conclusion of this work led to my being invited to take part in the re-enshrinement of the relics of the Buddha's two chief disciples, Sariputta and Moggallana, in the brand-new temple the Society had built for them at Sanchi, near Bhopal, not far from the stupa from which they had been removed a hundred years earlier by a British archaeologist. From Sanchi I went to Bombay, where I had been asked to advise on the production of a Buddhist film, and on coming to know that Ambedkar was in the city decided to go and see him.

Five years after independence Bombay was still a fine city. That is, it was a fine city if one confined oneself to the Esplanade and Marine Drive. Beyond these favoured regions stretched the densely populated working class districts of Bombay's industrial hinterland. Prominent among these districts was Dadar, and it was at the house that he had built for himself in Dadar that Ambedkar and I had our first meeting. On my arrival I was shown into a large, rather bare room that in the case of a modern British politician would have been called his surgery. A number of people were already present. After we had exchanged salutations and I had introduced myself (it was in any case obvious from my garb that I was a Buddhist monk) Ambedkar asked me to take a seat while he attended to some people who had come to see him. The people in question were the ten or twelve members of what seemed to be a deputation of some kind. As Ambedkar advanced towards them, a frown on his face, the three or four men in Western-style reach-me-downs who appeared to be the leaders of the deputation produced an enormous marigold-and-tinsel garland which they attempted to place round his neck. This token of homage Ambedkar thrust roughly aside with every mark of impatience, not to say irritation. Far from resenting this display of apparent rudeness the leaders of the deputation stood clutching the garland and gazing at their leader with an expression of utter devotion as, still frowning, he addressed to them (in Marathi) a few short, sharp sentences of what seemed to be rebuke. Evidently they had done something wrong, and he was scolding them. But they no more resented this than they had resented his refusal of the garland, the expression on their faces plainly saying that if instead of scolding them he was to beat them with a stick they would count it the greatest of blessings. This was my first experience of the devotion with which Ambedkar was regarded by his followers, and I never forgot that scene in the surgery. Indeed four years later it helped me to understand the readiness with which those same followers responded to his call to embrace Buddhism.

While Ambedkar was talking with the delegation (and eventually something seemed to be settled between them) I not only observed their reactions but also studied the great man himself. Ambedkar was of above-average height, brown-complexioned, and heavily built, with a distinct inclination to corpulence. His Western-style suit was well cut, but hung on him rather loosely, like the wrinkled hide on an elephant. As for his head, this matched his body, being large and well formed, while the pear-shaped face revealed an exceptionally lofty brow, very full jowls, a slightly aquiline nose, and a mouth the corners of which were turned down to a remarkable degree. More noticeable still was Ambedkar's expression, which was grim and lowering, as of a man who rarely smiled. So grim and so lowering was it, indeed, that watching him I had the impression of a great black storm-cloud—a storm-cloud that might discharge thunder and lightning at any minute.

This impression proved to be not without foundation. When the delegation had departed Ambedkar seated himself behind his desk and, after we had exchanged the usual amenities, fixed me with an unfriendly stare, and demanded belligerently, 'Why does your Maha Bodhi Society have a Bengali Brahmin for its President?' The word Brahmin was not only emphasized but pronounced with such contempt and scorn that the whole Brahmin caste, as well as any organization so misguided as to have a Brahmin for its president, was at once consigned to a kind of moral dustbin. Realizing that Ambedkar took me for one of the Bhikkhus (mostly Sinhalese) who ran the Maha Bodhi Society's various pilgrim-centres, I hastened to make my position clear. It was not *my* Maha Bodhi Society, I explained. Though I was happy to help the Society in whatever way I could, I did not actually belong to it, and one of the reasons I did not belong to it was that it had a Brahmin for its President, as well as a Governing Body that was dominated by Caste Hindus who had no real interest in Buddhism. Some of the Buddhist members of the Society, I added, were no more satisfied with the present state of affairs than he was and both they and I hoped that before long we would be able to do something about it. This explanation appeared to mollify Ambedkar, and the fixed stare became less unfriendly. For my part, I not only sympathized with his question but knew why he had asked it with so much feeling. Not only was the President of the Maha Bodhi Society a Bengali Brahmin, but that Brahmin was also a former President of the Hindu Mahasabha, a right-wing Caste Hindu organization. What I did not know at the time, however, was that Prasad Mookerjee—the Brahmin in question—had been one of the leading opponents of Ambedkar's Hindu Code Bill.

The air having been cleared between us, the conversation must have turned to Buddhism, for presently I asked him (probably with his article on 'The Buddha and the Future of His Religion' in mind) whether he thought that Buddhism really had a future in India. His answer to this question was an indirect one. '*I* have no future in India!' he exclaimed bitterly, his grim and lowering expression giving way to one so gloomy and despondent as to be akin to despair. But whatever he may have thought at the time (he had then been out of office for more than a year) fortunately there was, after all, a future in India for both Ambedkar and Buddhism, and when we met two years later this fact was already beginning to be obvious.

This second meeting also took place in Bombay, though not in Dadar but in the Fort area, at the Siddharth College of Arts and Sciences, an institution started by Ambedkar in 1946 mainly for the benefit of untouchable students. We met in his office on the top floor of Buddha Bhuvan, and on entering the book-lined room I found him seated behind his desk, with Mrs Ambedkar standing beside him. He did not look very well and apologized for receiving me sitting down. He was suffering from arthritis, he explained, and this made standing up difficult. Whether because he was in pain, or for some other reason, he was much quieter and more subdued than he had been on the occasion of our first meeting, and seemed to have lost much of his belligerence. In the course of our discussion, in which Mrs Ambedkar also joined from time to time, mainly in order to reinforce a point made by her husband, Ambedkar explained to me at length his plans for the revival of Buddhism in India, adding that he intended to devote the rest of his life to Buddhism. But though he had, as it seemed, made up his mind that he and his followers should embrace Buddhism, he appeared to be uncertain as to exactly how this was to be done. At any rate, he questioned me closely on the subject and I explained that formal conversion to Buddhism consisted in 'going for Refuge', as it was called, to the Three Jewels, i.e. the Buddha, the Dharma, and the Sangha, and in undertaking to observe what were known as the Five Precepts, or five basic principles of ethical behaviour. It was as simple as that. One could 'take' the Refuges and Precepts from any

Buddhist monk.

By this time Ambedkar and I had been talking a good while, and a feeling of warmth and confidence had sprung up between us, as though we were members of the same family. I was therefore not surprised when he asked me if I would be willing to administer the Three Refuges and Five Precepts to him and his followers. To this I replied that I would certainly be willing to administer them, but that their conversion would probably be taken more seriously by the Buddhist world if it took place at the hands of the oldest and seniormost monk in India, who to the best of my knowledge was U Chandramani of Kusinara, from whom I had received my own Shramanera ordination. At the time Ambedkar seemed not to pay much attention to this suggestion, but he must have given it further thought, for it was from U Chandramani that, ten months later, he took the Three Refuges and Five Precepts. Before we parted he did, however, ask me to write to him recapitulating everything I had said on the subject of conversion. He also asked me to speak to his followers and explain to them what conversion to Buddhism really meant. To both these requests I gladly acceded, and it was settled between us that I would write to him from Poona (where I was planning to spend a few weeks) and that a talk would be organized for me by his lieutenants in the city.

On New Year's Day 1956 I accordingly addressed 3,000 Untouchables, most of whom (I was told) were desirous of being converted to Buddhism, on 'What it Means to Become a Buddhist'. The meeting took place at Worli, a working class district situated south of Dadar, on a piece of waste ground adjoining some chawls or tenement blocks. Since many of Ambedkar's followers in the area were factory workers, and did not get home much before eight o'clock, the meeting did not start until quite late, and by the time I rose to speak there was a cold wind blowing, so that I shivered in my thin cotton robes. With the President of the Scheduled Caste Federation of Bombay for my interpreter, I addressed the gathering for over an hour, speaking as simply as I could and confining myself to fundamentals. Becoming a Buddhist meant going for Refuge to the Buddha, the Dharma, and the Sangha, I declared, as well as undertaking to observe the Five Precepts, but one could do this only if one understood what the terms Buddha, Dharma, and Sangha actually meant and in what the observance of the Five Precepts consisted. The Buddha was a human being who, by virtue of his own efforts, had gained the state of supreme spiritual perfection known as Enlightenment or Nirvana. He was not God, or the messenger of God, and he was certainly not an avatara of Vishnu as the Hindus believed. Going for Refuge to the Buddha meant resolving to attain Enlightenment as he had done, for inasmuch as one was, like the Buddha, a human being, one was capable of attaining what he had attained. The Dharma was the Teaching of the Buddha: the Teaching of the Way to Enlightenment—especially as embodied in such formulae as the 'three trainings', or Morality, Meditation, and Wisdom, and the Noble Eightfold Path. Thus for Buddhism the word 'dharma' had a very different meaning from what it had for Hinduism. In Buddhism there was no place for the caste system, or for Untouchability—which for orthodox Hindus were an integral part of their 'dharma' or religious duty. Going for Refuge to the Dharma meant studying the Teaching of the Buddha, understanding it, and practising it. In Buddhism there was no place for blind belief. A non-practising Buddhist was a contradiction in terms. The Sangha was the spiritual community of the Buddha's disciples, past and present, monk and lay, enlightened and unenlightened. Going for Refuge to the Sangha meant being receptive to the spiritual influence of those who were farther advanced upon the Path than oneself: it meant being inspired by their example and guided by their advice. As for the observance of the Five Precepts, this consisted in abstention from harming living beings, from taking the not-given, from sexual misconduct, from false speech, and from indulgence in intoxicating drinks and drugs.

Such was the gist of my remarks, as it was to be the gist of hundreds of other speeches I was to deliver to untouchable converts to Buddhism in the course of the next ten years. I did, however, seek to clothe the bare bones of my subject in a certain amount of living flesh in the form of illustrations and anecdotes. My poorly clad and predominantly illiterate audience followed everything I said with the closest attention and in a silence that was broken only by the applause that greeted any remark of which they particularly approved. Not unnaturally, the biggest applause was reserved for my comments on the subject of caste and Untouchability.

The third and last meeting between Ambedkar and myself took place eleven months later, about a month after the Nagpur conversions. Unfortunately, I had had to miss this historic ceremony, since the Indian Buddhist Society's invitation reached me rather late, when I had already accepted an invitation to give some lectures in Gangtok, the capital of Sikkim, and all I could therefore do was send a message of congratulation. Not long after giving my Gangtok lectures I went down to Calcutta, and from there left on a tour of the principal Buddhist sacred places with some fifty other 'Eminent Buddhists from the Border Areas' (as we were officially described) as guests of the Government of India. After visiting Bodh-Gaya, Rajgir, Nalanda, Sarnath, Kusinara, Lumbini, Sanchi, and Agra, as well as various dams and other industrial projects that the Government wanted us to see, we were taken to Delhi in time to participate in the 2500th Buddha Jayanti celebrations. On our arrival in Delhi I lost no time in going to see Ambedkar. Indeed, I not only went to see him but took with me as many other 'Eminent Buddhists from the Border Areas' as I could persuade to go. Most of them had not heard of Ambedkar before, but when I explained who he was, and how he had been responsible for the conversion of hundreds of thousands of people to Buddhism, they agreed that it was our duty to go and personally congratulate him on his great and historic achievement.

It was therefore with some two or three dozen colourfully clad monks, nuns, and laymen from Tibet, Sikkim, Bhutan, Kashmir, Ladakh, Himachal Pradesh, Darjeeling, NEFA, and Assam that I descended on Ambedkar's house in Alipore Road one morning in the second week of November. The sky was an unbroken expanse of brilliant blue from which the sun shone down with steadily increasing warmth. Since there were so many of us it was difficult for Ambedkar to receive us indoors, and chairs were therefore set out in the compound. Here the Eminent Buddhists from the Border Areas sat facing Ambedkar in a semi-circle, with the sunlight falling on the vivid magentas, oranges, and yellows of their robes. Ambedkar himself sat behind a small table, Mrs Ambedkar beside him. He wore a light tropical suit and a pith helmet and looked so old and so ill that I felt obliged to apologize for our troubling him, explaining that we had come simply to pay our respects and to congratulate him on his conversion to Buddhism. Despite the poor state of his health Ambedkar was obviously glad to see me again and glad to meet the representatives of so many different forms of Buddhism. When he spoke, however, it was in so low a voice that I had to come quite close to him in order to catch what he was saying.

In this way we talked for some ten or fifteen minutes. I then rose to say goodbye, the rest of the party rising with me. The purpose of our visit had been achieved, and in the circumstances it would have been inconsiderate for us to stay any longer than was strictly necessary. But Ambedkar would not hear of our going. Or rather, he would not hear of my going, for he had made no attempt to enter into conversation with any of the other Eminent Buddhists from the Border Areas. There was evidently much that was weighing on his mind, much that he wanted to speak to me about, and he had no intention of allowing bodily weakness and suffering to prevent him from continuing the conversation. The longer he spoke, though, the more concerned about him I became, for his head gradually sank until it almost touched his outstretched arms, which were resting on the surface of the table. Sitting there in that way, like an Atlas for whom the globe had at last become almost too heavy for him to bear, he spoke of his hopes and fears—mostly fears—for the movement of conversion to Buddhism that he had inaugurated. Once more, twice more, I attempted to bring the meeting to an end, especially as I could see that Mrs Ambedkar was becoming uneasy and that some of the Eminent Buddhists, not understanding what Ambedkar was saying, were beginning to show signs of restlessness. It was now the hottest part of the day, I expostulated; he had been sitting out in the sun for longer than was perhaps good for him, and we really ought not to trouble him any further. But the figure in the light tropical suit and the pith helmet refused to take any notice, though his head was now frankly resting on his arms and though the broken sentences came with increasing difficulty and at ever longer intervals. As I sat there, torn between my desire to let Ambedkar have his say and my fear that the continued exertion might do him serious harm, I had the distinct impression that he somehow knew we would not be meeting again and that he wanted to transfer to my shoulders some of the weight that he was no longer able to bear himself. There was still so much to be done, the sad, tired voice was saying . . . so much to be done. . . Eventually the great leader's eyes closed in sheer weariness and, seeing from Mrs Ambedkar's expression that it was time for us to go, I and my two or three dozen colourfully clad companions quietly filed out of the compound. My third and final meeting with Ambedkar had lasted exactly two hours.

From his appearance as he sat there in the blazing sunshine of that November morning I doubted if Ambedkar would ever set foot outside his house again, but a few days later he left for Kathmandu, where the delegates to the fourth conference of the World Fellowship of Buddhists gave him a tremendous ovation. For my part, having spent two weeks participating in the 2500th Buddha Jayanti celebrations I left Delhi for Bombay on 29 November—the day before Ambedkar returned from Kathmandu, as I afterwards discovered. In Bombay I stayed for only a few days, for though my friends there were hoping for a longer visit I was in a hurry to return to Calcutta, and on 4 December I accordingly caught the overnight train to Nagpur. Since I had been unable to attend the conversion ceremony on 14 October I was eager to make the acquaintance of the newly converted Buddhists there who had, in fact, already invited me to spend a few days with them on my way back to Calcutta and give some lectures. On my arrival in Nagpur the following day, at one o'clock in the afternoon, I found a crowd of some 2,000 excited ex-Untouchables waiting on the platform to receive me. After being profusely garlanded I was escorted to the house of the friend with whom I had arranged to stay and then left to rest there and recover from my journey. Less than an hour later, when I was still settling into my new quarters, there was a sudden disturbance outside and three or four members of the Indian Buddhist Society burst into my room with the news that 'Baba Saheb'—as Ambedkar's followers respectfully and affectionately called him—had died in Delhi the previous night. The speakers seemed utterly demoralized. What was more, they reported that the Society's downtown office was being beseiged by thousands of grief-stricken people who, knowing that I had arrived in Nagpur, were demanding that I should come and speak to them. Pointing out that it would be impossible for me to address so many people without a microphone and loudspeakers, I told my visitors to organize a proper condolence meeting for seven o'clock that evening. I would address it and do my best to console people, who from the accounts that now started coming in were frantic with grief and anxiety at the sudden loss of their great leader.

A condolence meeting was therefore held in the Kasturchand Park at the time indicated. When I arrived it was quite dark and the long columns of mourners were still converging on the place from all directions. They came clad in white—the same white that they had worn for the conversion ceremony only seven weeks earlier—and every man, woman, and child carried a lighted candle, so that the Park was the dark hub of a wheel with a score of golden spokes. Partly because of their demoralized state, partly because there had been so little time, the organizers of the meeting had been able to do little more than rig up a microphone and loudspeakers. There was no stage and, apart from a petromax or two, no lighting other than that provided by the thousands of candles. By the time I rose to speak—standing on the seat of a rikshaw, and with someone holding a microphone in front of me—about 100,000 people had assembled. By rights I should have been the last speaker but as things turned out I was the first. In fact I was the only speaker. Not that there were not others who wanted to pay tribute to the memory of the departed leader. One by one, some five or six of Ambedkar's most prominent local supporters attempted to speak, and one by one they were forced to sit down again as, overcome by emotion, they burst into tears after uttering only a few words. Their example proved to be contagious. When I started to speak the whole of the vast gathering was weeping, and sobs and groans rent the air. In the light cast by the petromax I could see grey-haired men in convulsions of grief at my feet.

It would have been strange if I had remained unaffected by the sight of so much anguish and so much despair, and I was indeed deeply moved. But though I felt the tears coming to my eyes I realized that for me, at least, there was no time to indulge in emotion. Ambedkar's followers had received a terrible shock. They had been Buddhists for only seven weeks, and now their leader, in whom their trust was total, and on whose guidance in the difficult days ahead they had been relying, had been snatched away. Poor and illiterate as the vast majority of them were, and faced by the unrelenting hostility of the Caste Hindus, they did not know which way to turn and there was a possibility that the whole movement of conversion to Buddhism would come to a halt or even collapse. At all costs something had to be done. I therefore delivered a vigorous and stirring speech in which, after extolling the greatness of Ambedkar's achievement, I exhorted my audience to continue the work he had so gloriously begun and bring it to a successful conclusion. 'Baba Saheb' was not dead but alive. He lived on in them, and he lived on in them to the extent to which they were faithful to the ideals for which he stood and for which he had, quite literally, sacrificed himself. This speech, which lasted for an hour or more, was not without effect. Ambedkar's stricken followers began to realize that it was not the end of the world, that there was a future for them even after their beloved 'Baba Saheb's' death, and that the future was not devoid of hope. While I was speaking I had an extraordinary experience. Above the crowd there hung an enormous Presence. Whether that Presence was Ambedkar's own departed consciousness still hovering over his followers, or whether it was the collective product of their thoughts at that time of trial and crisis, I do not know, but it was as real to me as the people I was addressing.

In the course of the next four days I visited practically all the ex-untouchable 'localities' of Nagpur and made more than forty speeches, besides initiating about 30,000 people into Buddhism and delivering lectures at Nagpur University and at the local branch of the Ramakrishna Mission. Wherever I went I repeated, in one form or another, the message that I had given in Kasturchand Park: Ambedkar was not dead and his work—especially the work of conversion—must continue. When I left Nagpur I had addressed altogether 200,000 people and the members of the Indian Buddhist Society assured me that my presence at such a critical juncture was a miracle and that I had saved Nagpur for Buddhism. Whether or not I had saved Nagpur for Buddhism it was difficult to tell, but there was no doubt that during those five memorable days I had forged a very special link with the Buddhists of Nagpur and, indeed, with all Ambedkar's followers.

It was a link that was destined to endure. During the decade that followed I spent much of my time with the ex-untouchable Buddhists of Nagpur, Bombay, Poona, Jabalpur, and Ahmedabad, as well as with those who lived in the small towns and the villages of central and western India. I learned to admire their cheerfulness, their friendliness, their intelligence, and their loyalty to the memory of their great emancipator. I also learned to appreciate how terrible were the conditions under which, for so many centuries, they had been compelled to live.

3

The Hell of Caste

Apologists of the caste system try to represent it in terms of a division of labour, as a force making for social stability and cohesion, and as a framework within which a rich and varied religious and cultural life can flourish. For the Untouchables, who occupied the very lowest place within that system, the reality was far otherwise. Speaking at the time of his conversion to Buddhism, Ambedkar declared that he felt as though he had been delivered from hell, and there is no doubt that the hundreds of thousands of Untouchables who followed his example felt similarly. The hell from which they had been delivered was the hell of caste, to which they had been condemned for centuries and which had inflicted on them, in the most systematic manner, what Ambedkar himself characterized as torment.

A clue to the nature of that hell is provided by the word 'Untouchable' itself. An Untouchable is one who cannot be touched, and he cannot be touched because his touch automatically pollutes the one who touches him or whom he touches. Such 'touch' is not limited to direct physical contact. Pollution can be transmitted indirectly, through the medium of an article with which Touchable and Untouchable are in direct physical contact, as when both stand on different parts of the same carpet, as well as through anything previously touched by an Untouchable. In particular, pollution is transmitted through food and drink. Contact is also held to take place, and therefore pollution to be transmitted, when the shadow, or even the glance, of an Untouchable falls on the Touchable's person or possessions. Indeed, contact with certain untouchable castes is so polluting that they are not permitted to approach within a certain distance of higher-caste Hindus (say thirty feet in the case of a Brahmin) or even to be seen by them. Thus the connotation of the term Untouchable includes 'unapproachable' and even 'unseeable'. Since contact with an Untouchable pollutes it is not surprising that such contact should be shunned and that to the Touchable or Caste Hindu the Untouchable should normally be an object of horror, disgust, contempt, and loathing. It is also not surprising that to the Untouchable the Caste Hindu, particularly the Brahmin, should be an object of fear and hatred.

But why is it that contact with the Untouchable pollutes? The traditional answer is that contact with him pollutes because he is a creature of filthy personal habits and low morals who moreover engages in unclean occupations such as the removal of faeces and the disposal of the carcasses of cows and other animals. Should it be further asked why the Untouchable engages in these occupations the answer is that according to the Hindu scriptures it is his God-given dharma or religious duty to engage in them and in no others. But what is it that makes him an Untouchable in the first place? To this most fundamental question the Hindu tradition makes an emphatic and unambiguous reply. The Untouchable is an Untouchable because he has been born of untouchable parents, i.e. of parents belonging to an untouchable caste, just as a Brahmin is a Brahmin because he has been born of Brahmin parents, a Rajput a Rajput because he is of Rajput parentage and so on. Having been born of untouchable-caste parents the Untouchable must live as an Untouchable and die as an Untouchable. Nothing can alter his position within the caste system. Even if his personal habits are immaculate and his morals irreproachable and he does not engage in any unclean occupation he is still an Untouchable and contact with him continues to pollute. Similarly, even if a Brahmin is of filthy personal habits and low morals and forsakes his God-given dharma of studying the Vedas he is still a Brahmin and his touch continues to purify. In the well known words of the sixteenth century poet Tulsidas, whose *Ramacarita-manasa* has been described as the Bible of the Hindi-speaking peoples of North India, 'a Brahmin possessed of all the vices is to be worshipped, and a Shudra endowed with all the virtues is to be despised.'

From the fact that one is an Untouchable because one has been born of untouchable parents it follows that according to Hinduism Untouchability is something that is inherited. The Hindu Untouchable is a hereditary Untouchable, and because he is a hereditary Untouchable he is polluted and polluting not at certain times of his life and under certain special conditions but permanently and under all conditions. He is untouchable in his very nature, and not only inherits his Untouchability from his parents but transmits it unimpaired to his offspring. But even though he himself is an Untouchable, could he not (it might be asked) at least marry a Touchable and thus ensure that his offspring were untouchable to a lesser degree, much as a black man might marry a white woman in order to produce lighter-coloured offspring? And could not those offspring in turn marry Touchables, so that in the course of a few generations the taint of Untouchability would be bred out of his descendants altogether?

Within the context of the caste system such a proceeding is quite impossible, even unthinkable. Though the definition of 'caste' (from the Portuguese *casta* meaning 'breed', 'race', or 'class') has been the subject of a good deal of discussion, and though it has been suggested that the word should be used as an adjective rather than as a noun, there is a general agreement that the most distinctive feature of the caste, or caste group, is that its members marry and give in marriage only among themselves. In the language of Anthropology, the caste (*jāti*) is endogamous, though the clans (*gotra*) of which it is composed are exogamous in that they intermarry, and must intermarry, with other clans within the same caste. A caste thus represents a combination of endogamy and exogamy. It is endogamous in respect to its relations with other castes, exogamous in respect of the relation of its constituent clans to one another. If one regards the exogamy as being more fundamental than the endogamy, and even prior to it, then one can speak of a superimposition of endogamy on exogamy.

Not only is there agreement that the most characteristic feature of the caste, or caste group, is that it is endogamous; there is also agreement that castes exist, and can exist, only in the plural number. Caste in the singular number is an unreality, even a contradiction in terms. This is because a caste defines itself, so to speak, through the relations in which it stands to other castes and in which they stand to it. A caste, or caste group, is a social unit whose members may or may not touch, may or may not intermarry with, may or may not eat with, members of other units within the same Hindu society. Above all, it is a social unit whose members think of themselves as being, both collectively and individually, superior to the members of some other social units and inferior to all the rest. This is why Ambedkar characterized the caste system as a system of graded inequality—though he might well have added that it was a system in which, while all were unequal, some were a lot more unequal than others. It was a system that comprised a congeries of hereditary groups, each adhering to its own God-given dharma or religious duty, whether that of a priest, a trader, an oil-presser, a potter, a weaver, a thief, and so on; each excluding the lower castes and in its turn being excluded by the higher castes, and each doing its utmost to protect and, if possible, extend its own social and economic interests at the expense of the interests of all the other hereditary groups. Thus the Hindus are not merely an assortment of castes but 'so many warring groups each living for itself and for its selfish ideal'.[1]

How many of these warring groups there are it is difficult to say. Some authorities speak of 2,000, some of 4,000, and some of 20,000, the discrepancy being mainly due to disagreements as to whether certain groups are castes or sub-castes. Whatever the

31

actual number may be, in principle it should be possible to organize all the different castes into a single, completely unified hierarchy wherein no two castes occupied any one grade, for in principle each caste is necessarily either higher or lower than every other caste. In practice it is not so easy to do this, since there are castes whose exact position in the caste system is a matter of dispute either between them and their immediate neighbours in the system or, as in the case of Shudras claiming to be Rajputs, between them and those supreme authorities in such matters, the Brahmins. But even though there is no completely unified hierarchy the lines of demarcation between the different castes are generally clear enough, and in the case of the major caste groupings they are very clear indeed. The thickest and blackest line of demarcation, perhaps, is that separating the Savarnas or so-called 'Caste Hindus' from the Avarnas or 'non-Caste Hindus'. The Caste Hindus, who are above the line, are those Hindus who belong to castes traditionally regarded as falling within one or another of the classical four Varnas or 'classes' (literally 'colours'), the four Varnas being those of the Brahmin or priest, the Kshatriya or warrior, the Vaishya or trader, and the Shudra or menial. The non-Caste Hindus, who are below the line, are all those Hindus who belong to castes other than the ones falling within the four Varnas. The Caste Hindus are synonymous with the Touchables, the non-Caste Hindus with the Untouchables.

Almost as thick and almost as black as the line of demarcation separating the Savarnas or Caste Hindus from the Avarnas or non-Caste Hindus are the lines which, among the Savarnas themselves, separate first the Brahmins from the non-Brahmins and then the Dvijas or 'twice-born ones' from the Ekajas or 'once-born ones'. The Brahmins are separated from the other Varnas, and indeed from all other Hindus, by virtue of the fact that theirs is the highest caste—or group of castes—and that, as the custodians of the Vedas and other scriptures, they are not only the teachers of the other castes but their ultimate authority in all matters relating to their social and religious life. The Dvijas or twice-born ones are separated from the Ekajas or once-born ones by virtue of the fact that they have been invested with the sacrificial thread. Investiture with this thread constitutes a second, initiatic birth and confers certain important privileges. Only those belonging to castes falling within the first three Varnas are also Dvijas, for only they are entitled to the sacrificial thread. Shudras, not being entitled to the sacrificial thread, are not Dvijas. The position of the Shudras within the caste system is therefore somewhat anomalous, since as Savarnas or Caste Hindus they belong with the Brahmins, Kshatriyas, and Vaishyas, while as Ekajas or once-born ones they belong with the Untouchables. According to Ambedkar the anomaly is due to the fact that the Shudras are the descendants of Kshatriyas who, as a result of their conflicts with the Brahmins, were deprived of their right to be invested with the sacrificial thread and degraded to a fourth Varna. The Brahmins were able to do this, Ambedkar points out, because they alone could officiate at the ceremony at which investiture with the sacred thread took place. Deprived of the sacrificial thread, the erstwhile Kshatriyas sank lower and lower in the caste hierarchy and eventually lost all their privileges. In modern times the Shudras, especially the so-called 'unclean Shudras', are virtually indistinguishable from the Untouchables.

From the lines of demarcation separating the Touchables from the Untouchables, the Caste Hindus from the non-Caste Hindus, and the twice-born Caste Hindus from the once-born Hindus, it is obvious that the caste system comprises four major caste groupings: the Brahmins, the non-Brahmin Dvijas, i.e. the Kshatriyas and Vaishyas, the Shudras, and the Untouchables. It is also obvious that, since the caste system is a system of graded inequality, the greatest inequalities will be those between the castes at the very top and the castes at the very bottom of the system, that is, between the Brahmins and the Untouchables. The Brahmins are the Bhudevas or 'terrestrial gods' and as such enjoy numerous privileges. According to the texts cited from various Hindu scriptures by the great nineteenth century social reformer Jyotirao Phooley, whom Ambedkar regarded as one of his three 'gurus' (the others being the Buddha and Kabir), 'The Brahmin is styled the Lord of the Universe, even equal to God himself. He is to be worshipped, served, and respected by all. A

33

Brahmin can do no wrong. Never shall the king slay a Brahmin, though he has committed all possible crimes. To save the life of a Brahmin any falsehood may be told. There is no sin in it. No one is to take away anything belonging to a Brahmin. A king, though dying from want, must not receive any tax from a Brahmin, nor suffer him to be afflicted with hunger, or the whole kingdom will be afflicted with famine. The feet of a Brahmin are holy. In his right foot reside the holy waters of all places of pilgrimage, and by dipping it into water he makes it [i.e. the water] as holy as the waters of the holiest of shrines.'[2] And so on. So holy is the water into which a Brahmin has dipped his right foot that the other castes can actually purify themselves by drinking it.

Thus according to the Hindu scriptures—scriptures composed by the Brahmins themselves—the Brahmins occupy an extremely exalted position. The position occupied by the Untouchables is one of corresponding degradation. If the Brahmins are the terrestrial gods and enjoy numerous privileges the Untouchables are the terrestrial devils and enjoy no privileges and hardly any rights. If the touch of a Brahmin purifies, contact with an Untouchable automatically pollutes, as the term Asprashya or '(hereditary) Untouchable' itself suggests, for it is because contact with him pollutes that he is an Untouchable and is so designated. Other designations for the Untouchables are hardly less opprobrious and hardly less indicative of the extreme lowliness of their position. They are Panchamas or 'fifth-class people', since they constitute a fifth class outside of, and separate from, the classical four Varnas; they are Antyajas or 'those born at the end', since they were born at the end of creation, after the four Varnas (the traditional account) or at the end of the village (Ambedkar's explanation); they are Atishudras or Shudras (menials) par excellence, and they are Pariahs and Outcastes—designations that are self-explanatory. From about the middle of the last century the Untouchables were referred to in Government literature as the Depressed Classes, which is what in the most literal sense they were, and from 1935 onwards as the Scheduled Castes. 1935 was the year of the India Act. In this Act provision was made for reserved seats for the Untouchables in the central and provincial legislatures, and the Government of India therefore attached to the Orders-in-Council issued under the Act a schedule or list of all those castes that were treated as untouchable. Thus the castes included in the schedule came to be known as 'Scheduled Castes' and their members are Scheduled Caste Hindus as distinct from Caste Hindus.

Another modern designation for the Untouchables is Harijans or 'Children of God'. This rather sentimental and patronizing term seems to have been coined by Mahatma Gandhi, but although enshrined in legislation it has found little favour with the Untouchables themselves, especially when used by Caste Hindus who, in practice, continue to treat them as Untouchables. On the same principle as that on which

a rose
By any other name would smell as sweet

Untouchability stinks in the nostrils of the Untouchables, as well as in the nostrils of all those who possess even the slightest vestige of human feeling, regardless of whether they are known as the Depressed Classes or the Scheduled Castes or even the Children of God. Whatever they may be called they are still Untouchables in the eyes of the orthodox Caste Hindus and contact with them continues to pollute.

But although Untouchability was the principal and, in a sense, the basic disability suffered by the untold millions of human beings who, down the centuries, occupied a position at the very bottom of the Hindu caste system, it was by no means the only one. The fact that they were Untouchables resulted in their being burdened, either directly or indirectly, with a wide variety of other disabilities as well. By the time Ambedkar was born some of the worst of these disabilities had, of course, been removed, though enough of them remained to cause him and his immediate followers serious hardship and suffering throughout their lives. Even today, thirty-eight years after the Constituent Assembly adopted clause 47 of the Constitution, the clause abolishing Untouchability, and thirty-two years after the Untouchability (Offences) Bill became law, the Untouchables continue to suffer at the hands of the Caste Hindus many of the disabilities imposed upon them by the Hindu scriptures. What is

35

hardly less disturbing, even the small number of Caste Hindus who are inclined to be critical of the caste system, and who believe that the Untouchables should be treated in a more humane fashion, continue to revere the very scriptures which uphold the caste system and which prescribe for the Shudras and Untouchables the most systematically inhumane treatment that one section of a religious community has ever inflicted upon another.

The disabilities imposed on the Untouchables were mainly social, religious, economic, political, and educational in character. Many of their social disabilities, in particular, stemmed directly from the fact of their Untouchability, for since contact with them automatically polluted there could be no question of social intercourse between them and the Caste Hindus and no question, therefore, of the two groups living together. In Ambedkar's own forthright words, 'The Hindu society insists on segregation of the Untouchables. The Hindu will not live in the quarters of the Untouchables and will not allow the Untouchables to live inside Hindu quarters. This is a fundamental feature of Untouchability as it is practised by the Hindus. It is not a case of social separation, a mere stoppage of social intercourse for a temporary period. It is a case of territorial segregation and of a *cordon sanitaire* putting the impure people inside a barbed wire, into a sort of cage. Every Hindu village has a ghetto. The Hindus live in the village and the Untouchables in the ghetto.'³ The location of the ghetto was often highly insalubrious. In the case of a village near Poona, which I visited in the early sixties, it was situated not only outside the mud wall of the village but on the very spot where the drainage pipes of the village discharged their effluent, so that the wretched inmates of the ghetto lived surrounded by streams of filth.

Since the village depended on the Untouchables for various services, such as the removal of faeces and the disposal of dead animals, it was impracticable to keep them permanently confined to the ghetto. Their freedom of movement was, however, restricted in various ways, so as to minimize the possibility of their coming into contact with the Caste Hindus. They were not permitted to use certain paths, or to pass through

the village at certain hours, especially at those times of day when
the sun was low in the sky and when the shadow of an
Untouchable could be thrown a long way. In some parts of India
they were not allowed to enter the village at all during the
daytime. What was more, they were not permitted to bathe in the
public bathing-tank or to draw water from the public well. They
were also prohibited from using metal cooking utensils, from
wearing decent clothes, and from wearing gold or silver
ornaments, all of which were the prerogatives of the Caste
Hindus. They were not even permitted to use proper Hindu
names, for Hindu names generally incorporated the name of a
god or goddess and for an Untouchable to be called by such a
name would bring pollution on the deity concerned and thus be
tantamount to sacrilege. The Untouchables were therefore
known by derisive nicknames or, in some parts of India, by the
names of birds and animals.

The religious disabilities of the Untouchables related mainly to
what became known, in modern times, as 'temple entry'.
Untouchables were not permitted to enter Hindu temples or
even, in some cases, to walk along the street in which a Hindu
temple was situated. Some untouchable communities possessed
small, insignificant temples of their own in which they
worshipped either the popular Hindu gods and goddesses or
quasi-tribal divinities peculiar to themselves. Brahmins did not,
of course, officiate in these temples. Indeed, the Brahmins and
other Caste Hindus could no more think of entering the temples
of the Untouchables than they could think of allowing the
Untouchables to enter theirs. Thus the Untouchables were
segregated from the Caste Hindus not only in the social but in
the religious sense. There was a temple—or temples—in the
village and there was a temple in the ghetto. The Untouchables
were not permitted, in fact, to participate in the religious life of
the Hindu community in any way. They were prohibited from
studying the scriptures, especially the Vedas, and from engaging
in the practice of asceticism *(tapasya)*. In this respect they were in
much the same position as the Shudras. According to scriptures
like the *Brihaspati-smriti* and the *Gautama-dharmasutra*[4] a Shudra
may not listen to the recitation of the divinely inspired words of

the Vedas, he may not recite them, and he may not learn them by heart. If he listens to them his ears are to be filled with molten tin or lac, if he recites them his tongue is to be cut out, and if he learns them by heart his body is to be split in two. As for the Shudra who engages in the practice of asceticism, the punishment that awaits him is sufficiently illustrated by the famous episode in the *Ramayana* in which king Rama, the divine embodiment of all the virtues, cuts off Shambuka's head for daring to engage in a practice reserved for the higher castes. The Shudras were, however, allowed to participate in the religious life of the Hindu community to a limited extent, even though their real religious duty *(dharma)* was to serve the three higher castes in various menial ways. They could, for instance, invite Brahmins to perform certain ceremonies for them and they could make offerings to the Brahmins. The Untouchables were denied even these doubtful privileges. Many of them, however, found consolation in the devotional mysticism of the great teachers of the Bhakti school, some of whom were themselves of low-caste origin and who were, more often than not, critical of the caste system and of the pretensions of the Brahmins. Among those who found consolation in this way were Ambedkar's own senior relations, for both his father's and his mother's family belonged by tradition to the Kabir sect, one of his father's uncles having in fact been a sadhu or wandering holy man.

The economic and political disabilities of the Untouchables were no less crippling than the social and religious ones. To an even greater extent than was the case with the Shudras, their condition was, in effect, one of economic and political slavery. The only reason they were not actually bought and sold in the market place was that they were, so to speak, public property and the Caste Hindus were free to make use of their services for whatever low and degrading purpose they pleased. As Ambedkar reminded an organization of Caste Hindu social reformers in a famous undelivered speech, 'Slavery does not merely mean a legalized form of subjection. It means a state of society in which some men are forced to accept from others the purposes which control their conduct. This condition obtains even where there is no slavery in the legal sense. It is found where, as in the Caste System, some persons are compelled to carry on certain prescribed callings which are not of their choice'.[5] The state of society referred to by Ambedkar certainly obtained in the case of the Untouchables. They were compelled to follow callings which were not of their own choice but laid down for them by the Hindu scriptures on account of their having been born in a particular caste. Besides being compelled to follow callings which they had not themselves chosen the Untouchables were also compelled to follow them on terms dictated by the Caste Hindus. Whether working as sweepers and scavengers or, as did the more fortunate among them, as landless labourers and tenant farmers, they were obliged to accept from their Caste Hindu masters whatever meagre recompense the latter were prepared to give them. The condition of the Untouchables was thus one of very real economic slavery and that slavery, bad as it was, was made even worse in modern times by the evil of hereditary indebtedness—indebtedness, that is, to the Caste Hindu moneylender. The Caste Hindus were able to keep the Untouchables in a condition of economic slavery mainly because the latter had no civic or political rights and because, being at the same time totally devoid of political power, they had no means of wresting those rights from the Caste Hindus. The condition of the Untouchables was thus one of political slavery, and because it was one of political slavery it was one of economic slavery too. Political slavery led to economic slavery, and economic slavery in turn reinforced political slavery, both these forms of subjection being sanctioned and, indeed, prescribed by the Hindu scriptures.

The educational disabilities of the Untouchables were the direct consequence of their social and religious disabilities. Contact with an Untouchable brought pollution, and for this reason the Untouchables were not allowed into the Hindu schools, which in any case were in effect Brahmin schools, being run by Brahmins—who were the learned class—mainly for the benefit of Brahmins. Another reason why the Untouchables were not allowed into Hindu schools was that the principal subjects taught in those schools were the Vedas and the subjects ancillary to the Vedas, such as grammar and prosody, and an Untouchable was not permitted even to hear the divinely inspired words of the Vedas being recited. The study of the Vedas was for the twice-born who, having been invested with the sacred thread, were alone eligible for such study. An Untouchable was not even permitted to learn Sanskrit, which was as much a key to knowledge in ancient and mediaeval India as Latin was in medieval and Renaissance Europe. Sanskrit was the language of the Vedas; it was the language of the gods *(devabhāsa)*, just as the script in which it was normally written was the script of the city of the gods *(devanāgari)*, and the very idea of an Untouchable speaking, reading, and writing Sanskrit was therefore an abomination.

The result of this policy was that for centuries together the Untouchables were kept in a state of ignorance and illiteracy that has lasted, for the majority of them, right down to the present day. In the Bombay Presidency Untouchables were first admitted into Government schools only about ten years before Ambedkar was born, and even then only in the face of strong opposition from the Brahmin teachers, who treated their untouchable pupils in the most humiliating fashion. They could not sit with the Caste Hindu children, they could not take water from the school water pot, and their teachers refused to mark their exercise books from fear of pollution. Some teachers even refused to cane their untouchable pupils, for caning them would mean coming into contact with them, even if only for a moment. They therefore hurled clods of earth at the untouchable children whenever they misbehaved.

Burdened as the Untouchables were with disabilities of this kind, it is hardly surprising that on the occasion of his conversion to Buddhism Ambedkar should have felt as though he had been delivered from hell—from the hell of caste, Untouchability, and subjection. It was also hardly surprising that, immediately after embracing Buddhism by taking the Three Refuges and Five Precepts, he should have formally abjured the Hindu religion, declaring, among other things, 'I renounce Hinduism which is harmful for humanity, and the advancement and benefit of humanity, because it is based on inequality, and adopt Buddhism as my religion.' It is interesting and significant that, at a time when Hinduism was not being exported to the West to the extent that it is today, Ambedkar should have renounced it because it was *harmful to humanity.* It was certainly harmful to the Untouchables. Just how harmful it had been for how many people and over how long a period it is impossible to tell, but writing in 1948 and referring to the schedule attached to the Orders-in-Council issued under the India Act 1935, Ambedkar comments, 'This is a very terrifying list. It includes 429 communities. Reduced to numbers it means that today there exist in India 50—60,000,000 of people whose mere touch causes pollution to the Hindus. Surely, the phenomenon of untouchability among primitive and ancient society pales into insignificance before this phenomenon of hereditary untouchability for so many millions of people which we find in India. This type of untouchability among Hindus stands in a class by itself. It has no parallel in the history of the world. It is unparalleled not only by reason of the colossal numbers involved which exceed the number of |a| great many nations in Asia and Europe but also on other grounds.'[6]

These 'other grounds' are the disabilities imposed on the Untouchables by the Caste Hindus and the sufferings that those disabilities entailed. At the time of Ambedkar's conversion to Buddhism in 1936 the population of (divided) India numbered about 400,000,000 of whom at least one eighth were Untouchables. Assuming the proportion of Untouchables to Caste Hindus to have remained unchanged for the last thousand or so years, that is, from the time of the decline and disappearance of Buddhism, then the total number of Untouchables who have been forced to live in the hell of caste must run into several hundreds of millions. This represents a truly appalling mass of human suffering, compared with which the sufferings of the blacks under white majority rule in America and South Africa, and even the frightful sufferings of the Jews under the Nazis, assume a temporary and local significance. Ambedkar himself spoke of the Untouchables as having undergone a holocaust, and a holocaust it indeed was in the metaphorical, if not in the literal, sense of the term. It was a holocaust that lasted for at least ten centuries, claimed several hundreds of millions of victims, and was conducted under the auspices of a religion that professes to see the Divine in every man.

Among the 429 untouchable communities enumerated by the schedule of 1935 there were many differences, including differences of size. One of the biggest of these communities was that of the Mahars, who were one of the two principal untouchable castes of the Bombay Presidency, the other being that of the Mangs. Though there were so many of them, and though in the Marathi-speaking parts of central and western India they constituted one tenth of the population, the Mahars were not concentrated in any particular place but scattered throughout the area now occupied by the State of Maharashtra. Every Hindu village had its colony of Mahars, who of course lived in the ghetto, and who besides serving the Caste Hindus in the usual way acted as watchmen and messengers. In return for these services they were given cast-off clothing and leavings of food, as well as being allowed to cultivate certain lands. These lands were known as watan. They had been granted to the Mahars by the Government in ancient times, and were exempt from taxation, but the fact that they held them by right of their services to the village meant, in practice, that there was no limit to the services they could be called upon to perform. Thus in addition to all the usual disabilities suffered by the Untouchables the Mahars lived in a state of actual serfdom. They were at the beck and call of their Caste Hindu masters at all hours of the day and night, they were not entitled to wages, and regardless of the amount of work they did they could ask only for a few rounds of unleavened bread or a few handfuls of grain by way of recompense. This state of affairs lasted well into the present century, the Mahar watans being abolished only in 1958, by which time comparatively few Mahars still followed their traditional calling.

The sufferings of the Mahars were especially severe under the Chitpavan Brahmin dynasty that ruled the Maratha empire during the eighteenth and early nineteenth centuries, first as Peshwas or prime ministers of the weaker descendants of Shivaji and afterwards in their own right. During this period the watan lands were taxed, the tax being payable in kind, and the Mahars themselves were compelled to go about with a broom tied to the end of their loincloth and an earthenware pot hanging from their neck. The broom was for covering up their footprints and the pot for spitting in, so that the feet of the Caste Hindus using the same road might not come into contact with anything polluting. Those Mahars who dared to rebel against the restrictions imposed on them, or even to raise their voices in protest, were liable to be trampled to death by elephants in the courtyard of the Peshwa's palace. Mahars could also be buried alive in the foundations of Caste Hindu buildings. Though the Peshwas were deposed after the Third Maratha War of 1817–19, the horrors of Brahmin rule were not easily forgotten. In the early 1850s a fourteen-year-old untouchable girl (not a Mahar but a Mang) who was attending Jyotirao Phooley's school for low-caste girls in Poona wrote an essay on the condition of the Mahars and Mangs. In this essay she observed, *inter alia:* 'Formerly we were buried alive in the foundations of buildings. We were not allowed to pass by the Talimkhana. If any man was found to do so, his head was cut off playfully. We were not allowed to read and write. If [Peshwa] Bajirao II came to know about such a case, he would indignantly say: "What! If Mahars and Mangs learn to read and write, are the Brahmins to hand over their writing work to them and to go round shaving widows [i.e. working as barbers, who were of Shudra caste] with their bags hanging from their shoulders?" God has bestowed on us the rule of the British and our grievances are redressed. Nobody harasses us now. Nobody hangs us. Nobody buries us alive. Our progeny can live now. We can now wear clothes, can put on cloth around our body. Everybody is at liberty to live according to his means. No bars, no taboos, no restrictions. Even the bazaar at the Gultekadi is open to us.'[7]

But severely as the Mahars suffered under Peshwa rule, there were signs that a new day was about to dawn for them and, indeed, for all the Untouchables of India. One such sign was the recruitment of Mahars as soldiers by the East India Company. Mahars continued to be recruited in this way even after 1858, when the government of India passed from the East India

Company to the Crown, and the practice did not come to an end until 1892. Whether under the Company or the Crown, service with the army made a tremendous difference to the lives of thousands of Mahar men, as well as to the lives of their dependants. They were liberated from the ghetto; they were provided with proper food and clothing; they were paid wages; they could even learn to read and write. Indeed, during the latter part of the century education was made compulsory for the children and other relations, both male and female, of all those in military service.

Among the Mahar families to benefit from these changes was that from which Ambedkar sprang. His father, his two grandfathers, and his six maternal great-uncles, were all military men, his father in fact being the headmaster of an army school for a number of years. Ambedkar was therefore born not in a ghetto outside a mud-walled village but in the midst of the garrison town of Mhow, where his father's regiment was then stationed. Since the family lived in the cantonement the young Bhimrao Ramji had little contact with the world outside the military area, and it was not until he was five years old that he had any personal experience of Untouchability. By this time his headmaster father had retired from the army and the family had moved first to Dapoli, in the Konkan, and then to Satara, where his mother died shortly after their arrival. In Satara they found that no barber was prepared to cut their hair (contact with Mahars brought pollution even to the 'clean' Shudra caste to which the barbers belonged), and Ambedkar's own hair used to be cut by his elder sister. He could not understand why, despite the presence of so many barbers in the town, not one of them was prepared to cut their hair. Questions of this sort disturbed him more and more deeply as time went on, and as one humiliating incident after another burned into his brain the consciousness that he was a Mahar and that for his Caste Hindu co-religionists contact with a Mahar brought pollution.

Years later, in a speech on 'Reasons for Conversion', Ambedkar declared that there were four or five incidents which had left a deep impression on his mind and led him to decide in favour of the renunciation of Hinduism and the adoption of some other religion. One of these was the haircutting incident. Another, which he also described, took place at about the same time, and may be called the bullock-cart incident. Ambedkar's father had gone to work as a cashier in Goregaon, leaving the children in Satara. One day he wrote inviting them to pay him a visit. The idea that they would be travelling by train to Goregaon thrilled the young Ambedkar greatly, since he had never seen a train before. With the money sent by his father they bought new clothes, and with his elder brother and sister he set off for Goregaon. On their arrival at Badali, the railhead for Goregaon, they found to their dismay that there was no one there to meet them, their father not having received the letter they had sent. Ambedkar's own affecting words best describe what then happened.

'Soon everybody departed and there were no passengers, excepting us, left on the platform. We waited in vain for some three quarters of an hour. The stationmaster enquired who we were meeting, what caste we belonged to, and where we wanted to go. We told him we belonged to the Mahar caste. This gave him a shock and he retreated some five steps backwards. But seeing us well dressed, he presumed that we belonged to some well-to-do family. He assured us that he would try to get a cart for us. But owing to our being members of the Mahar caste, no bullock-cart driver was willing to drive us. Evening was approaching and till 6 or 7 p.m. we did not succeed in getting a cart. Finally a cart-man agreed to take us in his cart. But he made it clear at the outset that he would not drive the cart for us.

'I had been living in the military area and driving a cart was not difficult for me. As soon as we agreed to this condition, he came with his cart and we, all of us children, started for Goregaon.

'At a short distance outside the village we came across a brook. The cart driver asked us to eat our food there for |since we were Untouchables| no water was available elsewhere on the way. Accordingly, we got down from the cart and ate our food. The water was murky and mixed with dung. In the meantime, the driver also returned after having his dinner.

45

'As the evening grew darker, the driver quietly boarded the cart and sat beside us. It became so dark, soon, that neither any flickering lamp nor any human being was visible for miles. Fear, darkness, and loneliness made us cry. It was well past midnight and we were frightened. So scared were we that we thought we should never reach Goregaon. When we reached a toll post we jumped out of the cart. We made enquiries from the toll-collector whether we could get anything to eat in the vicinity. I spoke to him in Persian. I knew how to speak in Persian and had no difficulty in speaking to him. He replied in a very curt manner and pointed towards the hills. Somehow, we spent the night near the ravine and early in the morning we set off again on our journey to Goregaon. At last we reached Goregaon on the following day in the afternoon, utterly exhausted and almost half dead.'[8]

But though the children had reached Goregaon, their troubles were far from over. A few days after their arrival the young Ambedkar, his throat parched with thirst, surreptitiously drank some water from a public watercourse. Unfortunately, he was discovered, and the enraged Caste Hindus gave him a severe beating.

By this time he had been admitted to the Government Middle School at Satara, and the reason for his being able to speak to the toll-collector in Persian was that he had been compelled to take that language instead of Sanskrit. Even in their high school days neither Bhimrao Ramji nor his elder brother were ever allowed to study 'the language of the gods'. They were Untouchables, and the Brahmin pundits simply refused to teach them. This was not the only bitter pill he had to swallow during his student days. He and his brother were usually made to squat in a corner of the classroom on a piece of sacking that they carried with them to school each day. The teachers refused to touch their exercise books, and some of them would not even ask the two boys to recite poems or put questions to them for fear of being polluted. Even when the family moved to Bombay, and Bhimrao was attending a leading government high school, the same cruel persecution continued. One day the teacher asked him to come to the blackboard and solve a problem. Instantly the class was in an uproar. The reason was that the Caste Hindu boys were in the habit of keeping their lunch boxes behind the blackboard, and the presence of an Untouchable so near the blackboard would have polluted the food and made it unfit to eat. Before Bhimrao Ramji could reach the blackboard and touch it, therefore, they darted across the room and threw the lunch boxes to one side. As though incidents of this sort did not make life hard enough for the sensitive boy, his teachers did their best to discourage him. One of them went so far as to tell him that education was of no use to him. After all, he was a Mahar, and what did a Mahar want with education? But the young Ambedkar, who was already beginning to have a mind of his own, angrily told the man to mind his own business.

Despite all difficulties, however, Bhimrao Ambedkar persevered with his studies. He passed the matriculation examination. He became a graduate. He went abroad. He attended two of the most prestigious seats of learning in the West and eventually, in 1917, he returned with a master's degree in arts and a doctorate in philosophy from Columbia University. But his difficulties were by no means over. In the eyes of the Caste Hindus he was still a Mahar and contact with him continued to pollute. Only a month after his return there occurred an incident that reminded him, in the most brutal fashion, that his position in Hindu society was exactly the same as it had always been. This incident took place in Baroda, and was another of those four or five incidents that left a deep impression on his mind and led him to decide in favour of the renunciation of Hinduism and the adoption of some other faith. It may be called the Parsi dharamsala incident, and Ambedkar described it in the same speech on 'Reasons for Conversion' in which he described the haircutting incident and the bullock-cart incident.

'With a scholarship granted by Baroda State, I had gone for education abroad. After returning from England, in accordance with the terms of the agreement, I came to serve under the Baroda Durbar. I could not get a house to live in at Baroda. Neither a Hindu nor any Moslem was prepared to rent out a house to me in the city of Baroda. Failing to get a house in any locality, I decided to get accommodation in a Parsi Dharamsala. After having stayed in America and England, I had developed a fair complexion and an impressive personality. Giving myself a Parsi name, "Adalji Sorabji", I began to live in the Parsi Dharamsala. The Parsi manager agreed to accommodate me at Rs. 2 per diem. But soon the people got wind of the fact that His Highness the Maharaja Gaekwad of Baroda had appointed a Mahar boy as an officer in his Durbar. My living in the Parsi Dharamsala under an assumed name gave rise to suspicion and my secret was soon out.

'On the second day of my stay, when I was just leaving for my office after taking breakfast, a mob of some fifteen or twenty Parsis, armed with *lathis*, accosted me, threatening to kill me, and demanded who I was. I replied, "I am a Hindu." But they were not to be satisfied with this answer. Exasperated, they began to shower abuses on me and bade me vacate the room immediately. My presence of mind and knowledge gave me the strength to face the situation boldly. Politely I asked for permission to stay for eight hours more. Throughout the day I searched for a house to live in, but miserably failed to get any place to hide my head. I approached my friends but all turned me down on some plea or the other, expressing their inability to accommodate me. I was utterly disappointed and exhausted. What to do next? I just could not decide. Frustrated and exhausted, I quietly sat down at one place, with the tears flowing from my eyes. Seeing no hope of getting a house, and no alternative but to quit, I tendered my resignation and left for Bombay by the night train.'[9]

One of the the strangest features of this incident was that Ambedkar should have been driven from a Parsi dharamsala by Parsis. The Parsis were not Hindus but Zoroastrians of Iranian descent, but owing to their long residence in India they had become deeply infected by the poison of the Hindu caste system. Though he did not mention the fact in his speech, during his brief stay in Baroda Ambedkar was not only driven from the Parsi dharamsala but, virtually, from his own office as well. His staff, including the peons, were all Caste Hindus, and even though they were his subordinates they treated him like a leper. Fearful that contact with him would bring pollution, the peons threw files and papers on to his desk from a safe distance. Drinking water was not available to him in the office. Thoroughly mortfied by the caste-ridden atmosphere of the place, Ambedkar was forced to seek refuge in the Baroda public library.

Incidents of this kind having led him to decide in favour of the renunciation of Hinduism and conversion to some other religion, Ambedkar naturally devoted much thought to the question of which religion would be the best for the Untouchables to adopt. Should it be Christianity? Or Islam? Or Sikhism? Or should it be a new religion, founded by Ambedkar himself? In the event he and his followers adopted Buddhism, but they did not do so until twenty years after his 'Reasons for Conversion' speech and twenty years after his description of the haircutting incident, the bullock-cart incident, and the Parsi dharamsala incident. The road to Conversion was not always an easy one, nor was it always clear. Yet looking back one can make out what seem, at least in retrospect, to have been milestones, some of them indeed going back to an early period of Ambedkar's life. These milestones were not all of the same kind, nor were they distributed along the road at exactly equal intervals. Some were not even very plainly marked, while others indicated the greatness of the distance that Ambedkar had travelled from Hinduism rather than the smallness of the distance that separated him from Buddhism. But all of them—and there may well have been others of which we have no knowledge—are important as illustrating the stages through which Ambedkar passed on the long journey that ended only when, on 14 October 1956, he went for refuge to the Buddha, Dharma, and Sangha.

4

Milestones on the Road to Conversion

Ambedkar's first recorded contact with Buddhism occurred in 1908, when he was sixteen. He had just passed the matriculation examination of Bombay University, and so extraordinary an achievement was this for an untouchable boy that the Mahars celebrated the occasion with a public meeting in his honour. The meeting was held in Bombay under the presidency of S. K. Bole, a well known social reformer from the Bhandari community who, some two decades later, was to co-operate with Ambedkar in the Chowdar Tank campaign. Among the speakers at the meeting was a local high school teacher called Krishnaji Arjun Keluskar. Though a Maharashtrian Brahmin by birth Keluskar was a man of liberal views and an admirer of the Buddha. He had, in fact, recently published a life of the Buddha in Marathi, and a copy of this work he now presented to the young Ambedkar. Being nothing if not an avid reader, the new matriculate lost no time in devouring the book, and there is no doubt that the sublime story of the Buddha's renunciation of all earthly ties, his search for truth, his eventual attainment of Enlightenment, and his compassionate activity on behalf of his fellow men, left an indelible impression on his mind. Keluskar, for his part, continued to take a keen interest in the brilliant untouchable boy, and it was through his good offices that, three years later, the Maharaja Gaekwad of Baroda granted Ambedkar the scholarship that enabled him to continue his education.

That a liberal-minded Brahmin like Keluskar should have written and published a life of the Buddha was a sign of the times. For at least seven or eight centuries Buddhism had been unknown·in India, the land of its birth, and the name of the Buddha himself had lingered on only as that of an alleged incarnation of the god Vishnu who had taken birth for the express purpose of misleading the asuras or anti-gods with a false teaching. But the darkness was lifting. Thanks to the labours of orientalists like James Prinseps and archaeologists like Alexander Cunningham, as well as to the more popular activities of the Theosophists, by the end of the nineteenth century the main events of the Buddha's career and the general nature of his teaching had begun to penetrate the consciousness of English-educated Hindus and, by their means, to percolate through the rest of society. In eastern India the founding of the Buddhist Text Society in Calcutta in 1892 gave an impetus to the scholarly study of Buddhism, while Anagarika Dharmapala's work for the resuscitation of Bodh-gaya, where the Buddha had gained Enlightenment, helped to remind people of the greatness of India's Buddhist heritage. The precise nature of Keluskar's relation to all these developments is difficult to ascertain, but it is clear that the worthy Brahmin was one of those who had come under the influence of the movement of Buddhist revival and that the book he presented to the sixteen-year-old Ambedkar was a product of that influence. Thus the book represented not only Ambedkar's first contact with Buddhism; it also represented his first contact with the movement of which he himself was to be the brightest ornament.

From 1908 to 1917 the future leader of the Untouchables was fully absorbed in his studies, first in India itself and afterwards in America and England, and during this period there was nothing to indicate that he was moving in the direction of Buddhism or even that he was giving any special thought to the Buddha's teaching. It was only in the middle and late twenties, after his second sojourn in England and his re-emergence into Indian public life, that there occurred any more of those incidents which, as we can now see, were milestones in his—and his community's—progress to Buddhism. But though Ambedkar may not have been moving in the direction of Buddhism during the period of his graduate and post-graduate studies he was nevertheless developing an outlook and even a philosophy that was, in certain essential respects, thoroughly Buddhistic. This was evident as early as 1918, when he wrote a review article on Bertrand Russell's *The Principles of Social Reconstruction*, published the previous year. Since the article was written for a journal of economics Ambedkar was obliged to confine himself to Russell's analysis of Property, but before dealing with this topic he discussed the question of how the philosophy of war was related to the principles of growth as expounded by the English philosopher. Characteristically, Ambedkar agreed with Russell that there is more hope for a nation that has the impulses that lead to war than for a nation in which all impulse is dead, observing, 'The gist of it all is that *activity is the condition of growth*. Mr Russell, it must be emphasized, is against war but is not for quieticism *(sic)*; for, according to him, activity leads to growth and quieticism is but another name for death. To express it in the language of Professor Dewey he is only against "force as violence" but is all for "force as energy". It must be remembered by those who are opposed to force [as such] that without the use of it all ideals will remain empty just as without some ideal or purpose (conscious or otherwise) all activity will be no more than mere fruitless fooling'.[1] This is very reminiscent of Buddhism's emphasis on virya, energy or vigour, as being indispensable at every stage of spiritual life. It is also interesting to find the youthful Ambedkar lamenting the prevalence of the 'philosophy of quieticism' among Indians, and rejecting the stock contrasts between the East and the West, bluntly declaring, 'Materialist we all are; even the East in spite of itself'.[2] He concluded this part of his article by quoting Bertrand Russell to the effect that every man needs some kind of contest, some sense of resistance overcome, in order to feel that he is exercizing his faculties, adding, 'in other words to feel that he is growing.'[3] Once again, this is reminiscent of Buddhism.

If contest and a sense of resistance overcome are necessary to human growth, then 1927 was certainly a year of growth for Ambedkar and his followers. 1927 was the year of the Chowdar Tank campaign, which at least in its opening phases was a complete success. The background of the campaign was what was known as the Bole resolution. This was a resolution moved in the Bombay Legislative Council by S. K. Bole, the social reformer, to the effect that the untouchable classes be allowed to use all watering places, wells, and dharamsalas which were built and maintained by Government or created by statute, as well as public schools, courts, offices, and dispensaries. After being adopted by the Council the resolution was accepted, with some reluctance, by the Bombay Government. Heads of departments were directed to give effect to the resolution so far as it related to public places and institutions belonging to and maintained by the Government, and Collectors were requested to advise the local public bodies in their jurisdiction to consider the desirability of accepting the recommendation made in the resolution so far as it related to them.

One of the local public bodies thus advised was the Mahad Municipality, and one of the amenities administered by the Mahad Municipality was the Chowdar Tank. This tank was a rectangular artificial lake of the traditional type, and the Caste Hindus were accustomed to draw water from it for household purposes. Untouchables were not allowed anywhere near the tank. Even when the Mahad Municipality, in compliance with the Bole resolution, threw the tank open to the Untouchables the latter were unable to exercise their moral and legal right to draw water from the tank owing to the hostility of the Caste Hindus. This state of affairs lasted for three years. Then in March the Depressed Classes of Kolaba district, in which Mahad was situated, decided to call a two-day conference to deal with the situation. The conference was held on the outskirts of Mahad, 10,000 untouchable representatives from all over the Bombay Presidency attended, Ambedkar delivered a stirring speech, resolutions were passed, and on the second day the conference formed itself into a procession which marched four abreast through the streets of Mahad to the Chowdar Tank. There Ambedkar, who was in the forefront of the procession, took water from the tank and drank it and the rest followed his example. Having thus demonstrated their right the processionists returned to the conference venue in the same peaceful manner that they had set out and started making preparations to leave for home.

They were not allowed to enjoy their victory for long. A rumour having gone round the town to the effect that the Untouchables were planning to enter the Vireshwar temple, a crowd of infuriated Caste Hindus burst into the conference venue and proceeded to belabour the delegates who still remained there with heavy bamboo sticks. Soon the whole town was in an uproar, and had Ambedkar not succeeded in restraining his more militant supporters a full scale riot would probably have ensued. As it was, twenty Untouchables were seriously injured, and numerous others were assaulted by gangs of orthodox Caste Hindus as they made their way out of the town. Belatedly, the police arrested nine of the troublemakers and three months later five of these were sentenced to four months rigorous imprisonment. Ambedkar remarked that had the principal officers of the district not been non-Caste Hindus justice would not have been done to the Untouchables, adding that under Peshwa rule he himself would have been trampled to death by an elephant.

But the Caste Hindus of Mahad were still far from having learned their lesson. In their eyes, as in the eyes of the vast majority of Caste Hindus throughout India, the action of the Untouchables in taking water from the Chowdar Tank had polluted the tank and rendered its water unfit for consumption. What had been polluted could, however, be purified, and what more effective means of purification was there than the five products of the cow, that is, milk, curds, clarified butter, urine, and dung? 108 earthenware pots of water having been drawn from the tank, a corresponding number of pots containing a mixture of these five products were therefore emptied into it to the recitation of mantras by Brahmins and the water of the tank was declared to be again fit for Caste Hindu consumption.

This so-called purification of the Chowdar Tank was deeply offensive to the Untouchables, and Ambedkar decided to continue the struggle and establish their right to draw water from the tank once and for all. In December of that year, after extensive preparations, a second conference was therefore called at Mahad. On this occasion 15,000 people attended, 4,000 of whom, in response to Ambedkar's appeal, declared their readiness to take water from the tank regardless of consequences. By this time, however, a group of Caste Hindus had filed a suit claiming that the Chowdar Tank was private property, an injunction had been issued restraining Ambedkar and his principal lieutenants from approaching the tank or drawing water from it, and the town was bristling with police. Ambedkar was in a quandary. On the one hand, he wanted to demonstrate the right of the Untouchables to draw water from the tank; on the other, he had no wish to break the law or antagonize the Government. In the end, after much anxious debate, a compromise was reached. On Ambedkar's recommendation the conference decided to postpone the struggle until the courts had settled the question of whether or not the Chowdar Tank was private property, but it also decided to go in procession to the tank and to march round it carrying banners and placards. The authorities having been notified, this was accordingly done and after Ambedkar had addressed a meeting of the town's Chamar or cobbler community the conference came to an end.

The right of the Untouchables to draw water from the Chowdar Tank was not finally established until 1937, when the Bombay High Court gave judgement in their favour. By that time the Mahad campaign had been overshadowed by other events. Even in 1927 itself, the first conference's action in taking water from the Chowdar Tank had been overshadowed, before the year was out, by the still more revolutionary proceedings of the second conference. That conference having repudiated those Hindu scriptures which preached the gospel of social inequality, and reaffirmed its opposition to applying them to the present social order, on the night of 25 December Ambedkar and his followers publicly and ceremonially burned one of the most celebrated of all such scriptures, the notorious *Manusmriti* or 'Institutes of Manu', which had governed the life of the Hindu community for fifteen hundred years and which, in the words of the conference, 'decried the Shudras, stunted their growth, impaired their self-respect, and perpetuated their social, economic, religious and political slavery'. It was one of the great iconoclastic acts of history, and the greatest blow orthodox Hinduism had suffered for more than a thousand years. So far-reaching were the consequences that Ambedkar's burning of the *Manusmriti* has been likened, by some of his admirers, to Luther's burning of the Pope's bull of excommunication against him. The comparison would have been still more apt if what Luther had burned at Wittenberg had been not the Pope's bull of excommunication but the Bible, for the *Manusmriti* was as much loved and revered by the Caste Hindus as it was hated by the Untouchables. Ambedkar himself, interviewed in 1937, emphasized the essentially symbolic nature of the burning of the *Manusmriti*. 'It was a cautious and drastic step,' he declared, 'but it was taken with a view to forcing the attention of Caste Hindus. At intervals such drastic remedies are a necessity. If you do not knock at the door, none opens it. It is not that all parts of the *Manusmriti* are condemnable, that it does not contain [any] good principles and that Manu himself was not a sociologist and was a mere fool. We made a bonfire of it because we view it as a symbol of injustice under which we have been crushed across centuries.'[4]

If the burning of the *Manusmriti* indicated how far Ambedkar had travelled from Hinduism, other incidents occurring in connection with the Chowdar Tank campaign showed how near he was beginning to draw to Buddhism. These incidents, which were three in number, were of a much less dramatic character than the burning of the *Manusmriti* and their significance was probably not appreciated at the time. Addressing the opening session of the first Mahad conference, Ambedkar told his poorly clad and illiterate audience, 'No lasting progress can be achieved unless we put ourselves through a threefold process of purification. We must improve the general tone of our behaviour, re-tune our utterance, and revitalize our thoughts.'[5] The threefold purification of which Ambedkar spoke was, of course, the purification of the three principles of body, speech, and mind, which between them make up the individual human being. What is especially noteworthy about Ambedkar's insistence on the need for a threefold purification is that whereas references to a threefold purification, corresponding to a threefold division of the individual human being, are found throughout Buddhist literature, they appear to be unknown to the Vedic and post-Vedic literature of Hinduism.[6] This suggests that even before the time of the Chowdar Tank campaign Ambedkar had not only familiarized himself with the Buddhist scriptures but had started thinking in specifically Buddhist terms. It also suggests that he saw progress not as simply material but as having a moral and spiritual basis. As the Buddhist scriptures make clear, the threefold purification is effected by abstention from the ten modes of 'unskilful' (i.e. ethically disastrous) action. Body is purified by abstention from killing, stealing, and sexual misconduct; speech by abstention from falsehood, abuse, idle chatter, and backbiting; and mind by abstention from covetousness, hatred, and wrong views. These ten constitute what are traditionally known as the 'ten precepts' *(dasa-sila)*, in their negative rather than their positive form, and it is not surprising that when, towards the end of his life, Ambedkar came to compile *The Buddha and His Dhamma*, he should have included in that work a number of passages from the Pali scriptures dealing with the threefold purification and the ten precepts. In the light of these facts one cannot help thinking that when Ambedkar told the first Mahad conference that no lasting progress could be achieved unless they put themselves through a threefold process of purification he was, in effect, telling them that no lasting progress could be achieved without Buddhism.

The two remaining incidents occurred in connection with the second Mahad conference. Two prominent non-Brahmin leaders of Maharashtra offered to support Ambedkar in his campaign on certain conditions. One condition was that no Brahmins, i.e. no liberal-minded Brahmins sympathetic to the cause of the Untouchables, should be allowed to participate in the campaign. Ambedkar flatly rejected the two leaders' offer. The view that all

Brahmins were enemies of the Untouchables was erroneous, he declared. What he hated was the *spirit* of Brahminism, that is, the idea that some were high caste and others low caste — an idea that implanted such notions as the pollutability of one human being by another, social privilege, and inequality. A non-Brahmin filled with ideas of superiority and inferiority was as repellent to him as a Brahmin free from the spirit of Brahminism was welcome. This noble and truly humanistic declaration showed that much as he and his fellow Untouchables had suffered at the hands of the Caste Hindus in general, and the Brahmins in particular, Ambedkar believed in seeing people not simply as members of this or that community but as individuals. In his eyes what counted was not birth but worth, and it was in accordance with the latter that men should really be judged. This was, of course, a basic Buddhist principle, and the fact that Ambedkar should have stated it so unequivocally shows how close he was, even at that time, to Buddhism.

But Ambedkar's closeness to Buddhism was not just in respect of certain principles; it was also a closeness of personal sympathy. In other words, the closeness was not only intellectual but emotional. Two days after the burning of the *Manusmriti* Ambedkar and his entourage went on an expedition to a place in the neighbourhood of Mahad in order to see the excavations of some ruins that were believed to date from the time of the Buddha. Deeply moved by the sight of the sculptures that had been unearthed, Ambedkar described to the members of his entourage how the Buddha's disciples had lived lives of poverty and chastity and selflessly devoted themselves to the service of the community. In a reverential mood, he asked them not to sit on the ancient stone benches that formed part of the ruins since these may have been the seats of Buddhist monks. It was almost as though he felt himself to be back in the days when Buddhism flourished in India and when Buddhist monks and monasteries were to be seen in every part of his beloved Maharashtra.

The six years that followed the Chowdar Tank campaign were years of vacillation. Sometimes it seemed that Ambedkar had travelled a long way from Hinduism, whether or not in the direction of some other religion, and sometimes it seemed that he had not. Sometimes he even appeared to be retracing his steps. Speaking at Jalgaon in May 1929, at a conference called by the Depressed Classes of the Central Provinces and Berar, he bluntly told his hearers that it was quite impossible for them to get rid of their disabilities so long as they remained in the Hindu fold and a resolution was passed to that effect. Fifteen months later, however, addressing the All-India Depressed Classes Congress in Nagpur, he declared that whatever hardships the Caste Hindus inflicted on him he would not abjure the Hindu religion. By 1933 the question of his abjuring Hinduism had become rather an academic one, for in February of that year he told Mahatma Gandhi that he could not honestly call himself a Hindu. Why, he demanded, should he be proud of that religion which condemned him to a position of degradation?

The truth of the matter was that for Ambedkar and his followers the question of their renouncing Hinduism was a difficult and complex one, with all kinds of social, economic, and political implications, and the untouchable leader tended to move nearer to, or farther away from, the taking of so drastic a step according to whether a change of heart on the part of the Caste Hindus seemed more, or less, likely. In the end, after years of unsuccessful struggle for the basic human rights of his people, he was forced to recognize that there was going to be no change of heart on the part of the Caste Hindus, and that the casteless, 'Protestant' Hinduism of which he had sometimes spoken so enthusiastically was only a dream. Indeed, it was a contradiction in terms. Hinduism and the caste system were inseparable, and since the outcaste was a by-product of the caste system—for where there were castes there were outcastes—it followed that there could be no emancipation for the Untouchables within the caste system and, therefore, no emancipation for them within Hinduism. If they wanted to rid themselves of their age-old disabilities they had no alternative but to renounce the religion into which they had been born.

As Ambedkar became increasingly convinced that renunciation of Hinduism was the way forward for him and his people the rumours began to spread, and in the summer of 1933 he had to assure an anxious correspondent that he was not about to become a convert to Islam. Writing from London, where he had gone as a delegate to the parliamentary select committee on Indian constitutional reform, he made it clear that while he was determined to leave the fold of Hinduism and embrace some other religion he would never embrace Islam ard was at that juncture inclined to Buddhism. A year later he was still inclined to Buddhism, for on the completion of the house that he had been building for himself and his books at Dadar he called it Rajagriha, after the ancient capital of King Bimbisara of Magadha, on the outskirts of which the Buddha had often stayed and where he had delivered some of his most important discourses. But much as Ambedkar was inclined to Buddhism, even at that stage, there could be no real movement in the direction of Buddhism or any other religion until he had definitely severed his connections with Hinduism. This dramatic step he was now about to take. The Caste Hindus having refused to change their attitude towards the Untouchables, the immovable object that was orthodox Hinduism was about to meet the irresistible force that was Ambedkar's determination to emancipate himself and his people, and when an immovable object meets an irresistible force there is bound to be an explosion.

The explosion took place at Yeola on 13 October 1935, and it rocked Hindu India in a way that even the burning of the *Manusmriti* had not done. The occasion was a conference which, it was announced, the leaders of the Depressed Classes had convened to review the social and political situation in the light of their ten-year-old struggle and the coming constitutional reforms. 10,000 Untouchables of all shades of opinion attended, including representatives from the Central Provinces and the adjoining princely states, and Ambedkar delivered a powerful and impassioned speech in which he described the hardships suffered by the Depressed Classes in all spheres of life, whether social, economic, educational, or political, and spoke bitterly of the failure of their attempts to secure their basic human rights as members of the Hindu community. The Kalaram Temple campaign, for example, had been a complete failure and a waste of time and energy. The time had therefore come for them to settle the matter once and for all. Since the disabilities under which they laboured were the direct result of their membership of the Hindu community, they should sever their connections with Hinduism and seek solace and self-respect in another religion. As for himself, it was his misfortune that he had been born an untouchable Hindu. *That* was beyond his power to prevent, but it was certainly within his power to refuse to live under ignoble and humiliating conditions. 'I therefore solemnly assure you,' he declared, 'that though I have been born a Hindu I will not die a Hindu.'

The effects of Ambedkar's declaration were immediate and far-reaching. Meetings were held up and down the country by various interested parties, statements and counter-statements were made, and Ambedkar himself was approached by all kinds of organizations and individuals in all kinds of ways. Not surprisingly, the most enthusiastic response to his speech came from the Untouchables themselves, for many of whom his promise that he would not die a Hindu carried a message of hope and deliverance. A few of them, indeed, acting on what they thought was a hint, at once became converts to Christianity, or Islam, or Sikhism, which was not Ambedkar's intention at all. The response of the existing followers of those religions was hardly less enthusiastic than the Untouchables' own. In some cases, it was even more enthusiastic. K. L. Gauba, a Muslim leader, telegraphed Ambedkar saying that the whole of Muslim India was ready to welcome and honour him and the Untouchables and promising full political, social, economic, and religious rights. Other Muslim leaders were no less pressing, and one of them—later reported to have been the Nizam of Hyderabad, 'the Richest Man in the World'—offered Ambedkar the sum of forty or fifty million rupees if he would undertake to convert the whole untouchable community to Islam. The Christians, who since the beginning of the last century had converted hundreds of thousands of Untouchables to their own faith, were not quite so straightforward. Asked what he thought of Ambedkar's declaration, Bishop Badley of the Methodist Episcopal Church, Bombay, replied that communities consisting of millions of people could become Christian only if their

61

members experienced a real change of heart. It was a change of heart that constituted conversion. All the same, he added, Ambedkar's statement would be welcomed by the Christian church, since it indicated that the Depressed Classes were ambitious for the better things of life and that a new era was about to dawn for them. On behalf of the Sikhs, Sardar D. S. Doabia, the Vice-President of the Golden Temple Managing Committee, telegraphed Ambedkar saying that the Sikh religion met the requirements of the Depressed Classes with regard to conversion. 'The Sikh religion', he added, 'is monotheistic and all-loving, and provides for the equal treatment of all its adherents.'[7]

A response to Ambedkar's declaration also came from the Buddhists, though unfortunately it was rather a mixed one. While the Burmese monk U Ottama, who was one of the leaders of the Hindu Mahasabha, condemned the renunciation of Hinduism by the Untouchables, representatives of the Buddhists of Burma, Siam, Tibet, and China who were assembled in Calcutta after the Yeola conference welcomed Ambedkar's decision and sent him a telegram inviting him to join the Buddhist community. The secretary of the Maha Bodhi Society, Sarnath, also sent a telegram. This read, 'Shocked very much to read your decision to renounce Hindu religion. Very sorry to read your resolution that Depressed Classes should break away completely from Hindu fold. Please reconsider your decision. I see untouchability is being brought to an end by thoughtful Sanatanists [i.e. orthodox Hindus] themselves. But if you still persist in embracing another religion, you with your community are most cordially welcome to embrace Buddhism which is professed by the greater part of Asia. Among Buddhists there are no religious or social disabilities. We grant equal status to all converts. There are no caste distinctions amongst us. We are willing to send workers.'[8] This rather ambivalent communication probably represented a compromise between the views of the Society's Bengali Brahmin president (not Shyama Prasad Mookerjee but his predecessor) and those of its Sinhalese Buddhist secretary. What Ambedkar thought of the telegram is not known, but he could hardly be blamed for thinking that the

Maha Bodhi Society would not be sorry if he did not 'persist' in embracing another religion.

The least enthusiastic response to Ambedkar's declaration naturally came from the Caste Hindus. Indeed the very idea that the most despised section of the Hindu community should have the effrontery even to think of renouncing Hinduism shocked and outraged them, and they at once took steps to ensure that the Untouchables remained within the Hindu fold. These steps consisted mainly in showering Ambedkar with abuse and his followers with promises that could be kept only by abolishing Hinduism—which the Caste Hindus of course had no intention of doing. The Caste Hindus were, in fact, as unwilling to allow the Untouchables to renounce Hinduism as Pharaoh was to allow the Israelites to leave Egypt, and for much the same reasons. If the Untouchables renounced Hinduism, and gave up their traditional occupations, the Caste Hindus would have no one to sweep and scavenge for them and would, moreover, be deprived of a valuable source of cheap and even unpaid labour. What was more, the renunciation of Hinduism by the Untouchables would drastically reduce the numerical strength and, therefore, the political power, of the Hindu community, and this would result in a corresponding increase in the political power of the Muslims, the Christians, or the Sikhs. Such a possibility the vast majority of Caste Hindus refused to contemplate. The only Caste Hindus to give even qualified approval to Ambedkar's decision to renounce Hinduism were some of the more far-sighted leaders of the Hindu Mahasabha, but even they gave their approval only on condition that Ambedkar and his followers embraced Sikhism, which according to them was a sect of Hinduism. As a matter of fact, Ambedkar was far more attracted to Sikhism than to either Islam or Christianity, and for a time seemed to be considering the possibility of adopting that religion.

Prominent among the opponents of conversion—even to Sikhism—were Mahatma Gandhi and other Caste Hindu leaders of the Congress Party. In a statement to the press, the Mahatma said, 'The speech attributed to Dr Ambedkar seems unbelievable. If however he has made such a speech and the

Conference has adopted a resolution of a complete severance |of connection with Hinduism| and acceptance of any faith that should guarantee equality, I regard both as unfortunate events, especially when one sees that in spite of isolated events to the contrary 'Untouchability' is on its last legs. I can understand the anger of a high-souled and highly educated person like Dr Ambedkar over atrocities such as were committed in Kavitha and other villages. But religion is not like a house or a cloak which can be changed at will. It is a more integral part of one's self than one's body. . . I would urge |Dr Ambedkar| to assuage his wrath and to reconsider the position and examine his ancestral religion on its own merits, and not through the weakness of its unfaithful followers.'[9] Ambedkar was as far from thinking that religion was like a house or cloak as Gandhi himself. When shown the Mahatma's comments he replied, 'What religion we shall belong to we have not yet decided. What ways and means we shall adopt we have not thought out. But we have decided one thing, and that after due deliberation and with deep conviction: that the Hindu religion is not good for us. Inequality is the very basis of that religion and its ethics are such that the Depressed Classes can never acquire their full manhood. Let none think that I have done this in a huff or as a matter of wrath against the treatment meted out to the Depressed Classes at the village of Kavitha or any other place. It is a deeply deliberate decision. I agree with Mr Gandhi that religion is necessary, but I do not agree that a man must keep to his ancestral religion if he finds that religion repugnant to his notions of the sort of religion he needs, as the standard for the regulation of his own conduct, and as the source of inspiration for his advancement and well-being.'[10]

The atrocities to which Gandhi and Ambedkar referred had taken place shortly before the Yeola conference. The Untouchables of Kavitha, a village in Gujerat, had decided to send their children to the local school. This was unacceptable to the Caste Hindus, who objected to untouchable children attending the same school as their own children and sitting next to them in class, and they vowed before the image of Mahadeva that unless the Untouchables withdrew their children from school they would enforce a strict boycott against them. The

Untouchables did not withdraw their children, and the Caste Hindus proceeded to carry out their threat. Untouchables were denied work as agricultural labourers, their cattle were prevented from grazing, and paraffin was poured into their wells so as to deprive them of drinking water at one of the hottest times of the year. In the end the entire untouchable community had to leave Kavitha. Neither the Government nor the Congress Party made the slightest attempt to intervene, though Mahatma Gandhi was ready enough with words of advice. Writing in his weekly paper *Harijan*, he observed, 'There is no help like self-help. God helps those who help themselves. If the Harijans concerned will carry out their resolve to wipe the dust of Kavitha off their feet, they will not only be happy themselves, but, they will pave the way for others.'[11] As a recent commentator caustically observes, 'Migration of Untouchables from Kavitha did not affect Hinduism or Gandhi's politics, so he advised them to quit Kavitha, but he dare not advise renunciation of Hinduism, because he loved Hinduism more than the poor helpless Untouchables.'[12]

Though according to Gandhi Untouchability was on its last legs this was by no means the case for, as Ambedkar grimly observed, 'Kavitha does not represent an isolated incident.'[13] Disregarding the opposition of the Caste Hindus and the objections of certain non-Mahar untouchable leaders, the great champion of the Depressed Classes therefore continued to follow his chosen path and reaffirmed his determination to renounce Hinduism from a number of platforms. Addressing the Maharashtra Untouchable Youths' Conference at Poona in January 1936, he declared that even if God himself was produced before him to dissuade him from leaving the Hindu fold, he would not go back on his resolution. Similarly, in his 'Reasons for Conversion' speech in Bombay three months later, in which he related some incidents from his own life which had led him to decide in favour of the renunciation of Hinduism and conversion to some other religion, he told his audience, 'If you continue to remain in the fold of Hinduism, you cannot attain a status higher than that of a slave. For me, personally, there is no bar. If I continue to remain an Untouchable I can attain any position that a Hindu can. . . But it is for your emancipation and advancement that conversion appears to be very necessary to me. To change this degraded and disgraceful existence into a golden life conversion is absolutely necessary. . . I have to start conversion to improve your lot. I am not at all worried about the question of my personal interest or progress. Whatever I am doing today, it is for your betterment and in your interest.' Then, in words reminiscent of the vows taken by the Bodhisattvas in the great Mahayana sutras, he concluded, 'You look upon me as a "God" but I am not a god. I am a human being like you all. Whatever help you want from me, I am prepared to give you. I have decided to liberate you from your present hopeless and degrading condition. I am not doing anything for my personal gain. I will continue to struggle for your uplift and to make your life useful and meaningful. You must realize your responsibility and follow the path which I am showing you. If you follow it earnestly, it would not be difficult to achieve your goal.'[14]

The most important of the meetings addressed by Ambedkar at this time was, however, the Bombay Presidency Mahar Conference that was held at Dadar, Bombay, on the last two days of May. The object of this conference was to decide how to implement the resolution that the Yeola Conference, following the lead given by Ambedkar, had passed seven months earlier—the resolution that the Untouchables should leave the fold of Hinduism. As Ambedkar himself explained at the outset of his address, he had called a conference of the Mahars rather than a conference of all the Untouchables for two reasons. Firstly, the question of what they should do for the betterment of their life was one that had to be solved by the different castes separately, through their respective conferences. Secondly, the time having come to assess the response of the untouchable masses to his Yeola declaration, the simplest and most reliable way of doing this was through separate meetings of each caste. Having thus cleared up any possible misunderstanding with regard to why he had called a conference of the Mahars, Ambedkar devoted the remainder of his 12,000-word address to an elaborate and well-considered statement of the case for conversion and, after urging the five hundred delegates to discharge their responsibility and decide whether or not to abandon Hinduism, concluded by giving them the message that the Buddha had given to his disciples shortly before his maha-parinirvana or 'great decease'. 'I have preached the truth without making any distinction between exoteric and esoteric doctrine', the Buddha had said; 'for in respect of the truths, Ananda, the Tathagata has no such thing as the closed fist of a teacher, who keeps something back. . . Therefore, O Ananda, be ye lamps unto yourselves. Be ye a refuge to yourselves. Betake yourselves to no external refuge. Hold fast to the Truth as a lamp. Hold fast as a refuge to the Truth. Look not for refuge to anyone besides yourselves.'[15] If they kept in mind these words of the Lord Buddha, Ambedkar told the delegates, he was sure their decision would not be wrong.

So great an effect did Ambedkar's address have on the conference that the delegates passed a resolution declaring that they were ready to change their religion *en masse* and that the Mahar community should, as a preliminary step in this direction, refrain from worshipping Hindu deities, from observing Hindu festivals, and from visiting Hindu places of pilgrimage. Nor was this all. Immediately after the conference Ambedkar addressed a meeting of Mahar ascetics at the same venue and these too decided to renounce the Hindu religion and, as though to demonstrate their determination, actually made a bonfire of the insignia of Hindu asceticism. Thus on that day—the second day of the Mahar Conference—there began the great movement of 'de-Sanskritization' whereby the Mahar community gradually severed its connections with Hinduism by discontinuing many of the traditional Hindu religious observances. On that day Ambedkar and his followers actually started travelling away from Hinduism. On that day they began the great march which, with every year that passed, put a greater distance between them and the religion that had inflicted on them such unparalleled suffering.

But despite the fact that Ambedkar had now started travelling away from Hinduism, and despite the fact that he had concluded his address to the Mahar Conference by quoting the words of the Buddha, he had apparently still not made up his mind which religion to embrace. When the flamboyant and eccentric Italian Buddhist monk Lokanatha interviewed Ambedkar in Bombay early in June, with the object of persuading him to become a Buddhist, all he could tell the press afterwards was that he believed he had succeeded in convincing Dr Ambedkar that if the Harijans agreed to their conversion to the Buddhist faith they would raise themselves morally, spiritually, and socially and attain a higher status in society. Dr Ambedkar had seemed to be impressed with the Buddhist faith, the monk added, and had promised to consider the question carefully. He had not, however, given any definite reply. Nevertheless, even though the untouchable leader had not yet decided which religion to embrace, and was not to give 'a definite reply' to questions on the subject for some years to come, there were signs that he continued to be mentally preoccupied with Buddhism and was, perhaps, inclining more and more to that religion. Addressing a meeting of the Depressed Classes at Bandra, Bombay, in August 1937, he again quoted from the words of the Buddha, telling his hearers that they should adopt another religion only after testing it as gold is tested in the fire. Similarly, speaking to the Christians of Sholapur in January 1938 he declared that he could say from his study of comparative religion that only two personalities had been able to captivate him: the Buddha and Christ. In South India, however, the caste system was observed in the Christian churches, and the Christians as a community had never fought for the removal of social injustice.

On 1—3 September 1939 World War II broke out in Europe and soon involved India, and on 15 August 1947 a truncated India achieved independence. During the eight years spanned by these events Ambedkar reached the zenith of his political career, first as Labour Member of the Viceroy's Executive Council, then as a member of the Constituent Assembly, and finally as Minister for Law in the first government of free India. Since he also continued to play a leading part in the affairs of the Depressed Classes and to work for the social, economic, political, and educational advancement of its members, there was no question of his being able to move very far in the direction of conversion, which he of course saw as concerning not just himself personally, but the whole untouchable community. Even during this period, however, there were indications that he remained preoccupied with Buddhism. In February 1940 he told the representative of a Bombay newspaper that Untouchability was originally imposed as a punishment for sticking to Buddhism when others had deserted it—a thesis he was to develop in his book *The Untouchables,* published in 1948. The villains of the piece were, of course, the Brahmins. In September 1944, speaking in a similar vein, he told a public meeting held under the auspices of the Madras Rationalist Society that the fundamental fact of ancient Indian history was that there had been a great struggle between Buddhism, which had ushered in a revolution, and Brahminism, which had launched a counter-revolution. The quarrel was over a single issue: 'What is Truth?' According to the Buddha, Truth was something that was borne witness to by one's own human faculties, physical and mental, whereas according to Brahminism it was something that was declared by the divinely revealed Vedas. In November 1945 the pandal in which Ambedkar addressed the Provincial Conference of the Scheduled Caste Federation, held in Ahmedabad on the banks of the river Sabarmati, was called Buddhanagar or 'City of the Buddha', while in June the following year he himself gave the college that the People's Education Society had started in Bombay the name of Siddharth College, Siddhartha (or Siddhattha) being the personal name of the Buddha. What was perhaps of greater significance, in 1948 he brought out a new edition of P. Lakshmi Narasu's *The Essence of Buddhism,* originally published in 1907. In the preface he wrote for it he praised the author for his unflagging faith in the Buddha and recommended his book as 'the best book on Buddhism that has appeared so far'.[16] He also revealed that he was himself working on a Life of the Buddha, in which he intended to deal with some of the criticisms that had been levelled against the teachings of the Buddha by his adversaries—past and present.

This Life of the Buddha must have been the work that was eventually published under the title of *The Buddha and His Dhamma,* and the fact that Ambedkar engaged on it while still a member of the Cabinet showed that he was more preoccupied with Buddhism than ever. So preoccupied was he, indeed, that speaking in the Constituent Assembly in November 1949 he could not forbear observing, 'It is not that India did not know parliaments or parliamentary procedure. A study of the Buddhist Bhikshu Sanghas discloses that there were parliaments—for the Sanghas were nothing but parliaments—but [that] the Sanghas knew and observed all the rules of parliamentary procedure known to modern times. They had rules regarding seating arrangements, rules regarding motions, resolutions, quorum, whip, counting of votes, voting by ballot, censure motion, regularization, res judicata etc. Although these rules of parliamentary procedure were applied by the Buddha to the meetings of the Bhikshu Sanghas, he must have borrowed them from the rules of the political assemblies functioning in the country in his time.'[17] Out of the abundance of the heart the mouth speaketh! Ambedkar had clearly been making a close study of the Vinaya-Pitaka or 'Book of the Discipline' (a study the fruits of which are visible in *The Buddha and His Dhamma*, Books I and IV), and it was no doubt partly as a result of his study of the Buddhist scriptures that he was now definitely inclined to Buddhism and had, in fact, more or less made up his mind to embrace that religion.

It was therefore not surprising that on 2 May 1950 he should have delivered at the Buddha Vihara, New Delhi, a speech that the press, at least, took to be a call to India's 70,000,000 'Harijans' to embrace Buddhism and which it therefore described as 'a dramatic development of great national importance and interest through south-east Asia'.[18] In the course of this speech, given on the occasion of the anniversary of the Buddha's attainment of Enlightenment, Ambedkar declared that neither Rama nor Krishna could be compared to the Buddha, that it was impossible for the Untouchables to love Hinduism, which had deprived them of all their rights, that a religion should be examined rationally before acceptance, and that without religion society would perish. Later he told a reporter that he was 'on his way to embrace Buddhism'—a statement that defined his position with lawyer-like precision. The following day, in Bombay, he was somewhat more forthcoming. He had been a student of

Buddhism for several years, he told the *Times of India*, though it might not be entirely correct to describe him as a Buddhist. As for his having called on the Scheduled Caste community to embrace Buddhism, he had not done so. Again his statement defined his position with lawyer-like precision, for if it was not entirely correct to describe him as a Buddhist it followed that it was not entirely correct to describe him as not a Buddhist. As he had said the day before, he was on his way to embracing Buddhism.

Thus Ambedkar's position with respect to Buddhism was quite clear. A week later, however, P. N. Rajbhoj, the General Secretary of the All-India Scheduled Caste Federation, issued a statement to the press saying that following certain controversies regarding Dr Ambedkar's advice to the Scheduled Caste community to embrace Buddhism he had had a long talk with Dr Ambedkar and that it appeared to him that Dr Ambedkar was of the opinion that the entire Hindu community should adopt Buddhism and not just the Scheduled Castes, since Hinduism 'tended to perpetuate vested interests and was utterly unsuitable in the present set-up when all people demanded equal opportunity and freedom'.[18] This statement only served to create fresh confusion, and the press complained that it was a mystery why India's Law Minister should allow his followers to interpret his views on important subjects instead of openly expressing his attitude. Yet in reality there was no mystery, for there was no inconsistency between Rajbhoj's statement and Ambedkar's declared position. Ambedkar was on his way to embracing Buddhism, and Rajbhoj's statement amounted to no more than saying that the great leader wanted to take with him as many people as possible. That such was indeed the case was evident from an article on 'The Buddha and the Future of His Religion' which Ambedkar contributed to the April-May issue of the *Maha Bodhi*, the journal of the Maha Bodhi Society. In this important article, which showed how deeply he had been thinking about Buddhism, Ambedkar even went so far as to declare that Buddhism was the only religion which the world could have. 'If the new world—which be it realized is very different from the old—must have a religion—and the new world needs a religion far more than the old world did—then it can only be the religion

71

of the Buddha.'[20]

But whatever 'mystery' there might be about whether or not Ambedkar was on his way to Buddhism, there could be no doubt, even in the minds of newspaper editors, that he was on his way to Ceylon (Sri Lanka). On 25 May he arrived in Colombo by air with his wife and Rajbhoj and the same day attended the inaugural meeting of the World Fellowship of Buddhists at the Temple of the Tooth in Kandy. Since he was not attending the meeting as a delegate (for that would have implied that he considered himself a Buddhist), he declined to speak at the official session and, instead, addressed the delegates after they had adopted the resolution inaugurating the Fellowship. There were people in India, he told them, who thought that the time had come when the effort might be made to revive Buddhism, and one of the objects of his visit was to observe Buddhist ceremonies and rituals, which the people of India had no means of witnessing. Another object was to find out to what extent Buddhism was practised in its pristine purity and to what extent its teachings had been encrusted with beliefs incompatible with its basic principles. He was also interested in finding out to what extent the religion of the Buddha was 'a live thing' and whether it existed merely because the people of Ceylon happened to be Buddhists in the traditional sense of the word. Having thus explained the purpose of his visit, Ambedkar turned to the conference itself. He was not fully satisfied, he said, with the resolution that had been passed calling for a World *Fellowship* of Buddhists. What was wanted was a declaration on the part of all the Buddhist countries that they were determined not merely to have a Fellowship but that they would propagate the religion and make sacrifices for it. Whether the delegates realized it or not, what Ambedkar was really saying was that the Buddhist countries of Asia should be less inward-looking and more outward-looking.

He himself was, as usual, sufficiently outward-looking. After the conclusion of the conference he not only saw as much as he could of the ceremonies and rituals of Ceylon Buddhism but found time to address the Young Men's Buddhist Association, Colombo, on 'The Rise and Fall of Buddhism in India'. Buddhism

72

had not disappeared from India, he asserted. Though its material form had disappeared, as a spiritual force it still existed. What had led to the decline of Buddhism in India was not clear. He himself was still studying the subject, but he believed that Buddhism had faded away in India because of the rise of Vaishnavism and Shivaism and because of the Muslim invasion of India. 'When Alla-ud-din marched into Bihar, he killed five to six thousand Bhikkhus. The remaining Buddhist monks fled to neighbouring countries like China, Nepal, and Tibet. Efforts were, subsequently, made by Buddhists of India to raise another priesthood in order to revive Buddhism. But these failed as by then ninety per cent of the people had embraced Hinduism.' Answering the question why Hinduism had survived in India and Buddhism had died, Ambedkar observed, 'Buddhism as a religion is difficult to practise while Hinduism is not.'[21] Shortly afterwards he addressed a meeting in the Colombo Town Hall and appealed to the Untouchables there to embrace Buddhism, saying that there was no need for them to have a separate organization. He also urged the Buddhists of Ceylon to accept the Untouchables and look after their interests with paternal care.

Ambedkar's visit to Ceylon naturally attracted a good deal of attention, and on his return to India some of his opponents accused him of being an opportunist. Replying to the charge in the course of a speech delivered under the auspices of the Bombay Branch of the Royal Asiatick Society on 25 July he denied that he was an opportunist with regard to his views on Buddhism and said that he had been interested in Buddhism since his boyhood. Later in the year, on 29 September, he returned to the question of conversion in a way that showed how broad was his vision and how much he had the welfare of the whole country at heart. Speaking at the Japanese Buddhist Temple, Worli (Bombay), he deprecated the idea that political independence meant the end of all the country's ills. So long as there was no purity, wrongdoing and utter disregard of morals would continue in everyday life; and as long as man did not know how to behave with man, India could never be prosperous. 'To end all these troubles, India must embrace Buddhism', he declared. 'Buddhism is the only religion based upon ethical principles and teaches how to work for the wellbeing of the common man.'[22] As if to underline the urgency of the situation, he concluded his speech by declaring that he would devote the rest of his life to the revival and spread of Buddhism.

This was more easily said than done. As Minister for Law, Ambedkar was responsible for piloting the Hindu Code Bill through the Constituent Assembly, besides which the poor state of his health was giving increasing cause for concern. But though he was not, as yet, able to devote himself to the revival and spread of Buddhism his mind was made up, and speaking at the Buddha Vihara, New Delhi, in May 1951, he declared, 'If the rest of the Hindu society does not co-operate, then we, the members of the Scheduled Castes, will go on our own and try once again to bring back Buddhism to its former glory and prestige in this country.'[23] Buddhism could not be restored to its former glory, however, whether by the members of the Scheduled Castes or anyone else, so long as the charges that were often levelled against it were allowed to remain unanswered. A Hindu author writing in *Eve's Weekly* having claimed that it was the Buddhist theory that had first thrust women into the background and that the Buddha was ever exhorting men to beware of women, Ambedkar therefore contributed to the April—May issue of the *Maha Bodhi* a pungent and scholarly article entitled 'The Rise and Fall of the Hindu Woman. Who was Responsible for it?' In this article he showed conclusively that it was not the Buddha who was responsible for the downfall of the Hindu woman but the Hindu law-giver Manu, the author of the *Manusmriti*. According to Ambedkar, the Buddha endeavoured to ennoble woman and raise her to the level of man.

July saw the formation of the Indian Buddhist Society, and in September Ambedkar told the Constituent Assembly, in the course of a speech on the Hindu Code Bill, 'The Buddha preached equality. He was the greatest opponent of the chaturvarnya*; he was the greatest opponent of belief in the

*The theory of the division of society into four classes: Brahmins (priests), Kshatruyas (warriors), Vaishyas (traders), and Shudras (menials).

Vedas because he believed in reason and did not believe in the infallibility of any book. He believed in ahimsa. Brahminic society accepted [only] the most innocuous dogma of ahimsa. They were never able to accept, in fact they opposed, his belief in equality. That is why Hindu society has remained what it always has been.'[24] A week later, on 29 September 1951, the Hindu Code Bill was killed even in the truncated form of a Marriage and Divorce Bill and Ambedkar resigned from the Nehru Cabinet.

But though he was no longer a member of the Government, Ambedkar continued to play a prominent role in the political life of the country, both inside and outside the Constituent Assembly, and continued to express unpopular opinions from a variety of platforms. In February 1953, speaking at a reception given in honour of M. R. Murti, the Vice-President of the Indo-Japanese Cultural Association in Japan, he declared, 'In the present condition of the world, so far as I have been able to study the situation, I have come to the conclusion that the conflict, whatever form it may take, will ultimately be between the Gospel of the Buddha and the Gospel of Karl Marx.'[25] It was from that point of view, he added, that he had been attracted by Japan, by China, and by other Eastern countries. Two months later, on the occasion of his sixty-second birthday, when a mile-long procession was taken out through the streets of Bombay in his honour, he told journalists that he would devote the rest of his life to the welfare of the Scheduled Castes people and the study of Buddhism. This assurance he repeated the following month, when presiding over a meeting organized by the Scheduled Caste Federation to celebrate the anniversary of the Buddha's attainment of Enlightenment. There would be no progress in the country, he told his 5,000 strong audience, unless a classless and casteless society was created. There would be no improvement in the lot of the Depressed Classes so long as they remained within the Hindu fold. He was glad to note that (Caste) Hindus, too, were participating in the celebration in large numbers. Buddhism would spread rapidly in India, and he was going to devote the rest of his life to propagating its teachings.

By this time India's first general election had come and gone, the Congress Party had swept the polls, and Ambedkar had failed to gain a seat in the Lok Sabha. Though he subsequently became a member of the Rajya Sabha, and took an active part in its proceedings for the rest of his life, his political career was now virtually over and he was at last free to devote himself to spreading Buddhism. In May 1954 he spent two weeks in Burma, attending the annual Vaisakha celebrations, in June he announced that he was starting a seminary in Bangalore to train preachers for the propagation of Buddhism in India, and in August, in the course of an important speech on India's foreign policy, he not only warned the Government of the possibility of Chinese aggression but criticized Chairman Mao for the way in which he treated the Buddhists of China. October saw Ambedkar in the role of broadcaster. Speaking on All-India Radio in the series 'My Personal Philosophy', he declared, 'Positively, my social philosophy may be said to be enshrined in three words: liberty, equality, and fraternity. Let no one however say that I have borrowed my philosophy from the French Revolution. I have not. My philosophy has roots in religion and not in political science. I have derived them from the teachings of my master, the Buddha'.[26]

In December he was again in Burma, this time in connection with the Third Conference of the World Fellowship of Buddhists which was being held in Rangoon. Addressing the Conference, he said, 'I have to say this with great anguish, that in the land where the Great Buddha was born his religion has declined. How such a thing happened is beyond anyone's comprehension.' As he spoke, his eyes filled with tears and for a few minutes he was unable to proceed with his speech. Later, he gave a resumé of his plans for the revival of Buddhism in India, adding that the enormous sums of money that the Buddhists of Ceylon and Burma spent on decorating their shrines on the occasion of religious festivals could be more usefully devoted to the propagation of Buddhism in other countries. After the Conference the delegates were taken to see Mandalay, formerly the capital of Upper Burma. Here Ambedkar stayed for a week and here, according to one account, he decided that he and his followers would formally embrace Buddhism in the 2500th year of the Buddhist era, i.e. in 1956—57. Even if such a decision actually was taken, however, no announcement of the fact was made either then or after Ambedkar's return to India, though an article by Dr R. L. Soni, an Indian medical man with whom Ambedkar had stayed in Mandalay, appeared in a Burmese newspaper under the heading 'An Open Invitation to the Scheduled Caste Indians'. In this article the doctor, who was himself a Buddhist, called upon his outcaste fellow countrymen to embrace Buddhism. 'The moment you come under the benevolent refuge of the All-Compassionate Buddha,' he assured them, 'your eyes shall twinkle with a new brilliance, your heart shall register the first throb of an experience of real social freedom and your mind shall know the impulse of a joy that is beyond the ken of words.'[27]

Five months after his visit to Burma Ambedkar re-formed and registered the Indian Buddhist Society, and seven months later, on 25 December 1955, he installed an image of the Buddha with which he had been presented in Rangoon in a temple built by members of the Scheduled Caste community at Dehu Road, near Poona. 1,200 years after the fall of Buddhism, he told the 4,000 men, women, and children who had gathered to hear him, the honour of establishing the image of the Lord Buddha had fallen to his people. It was a great event, and would undoubtedly go down in history. As for his personal intentions, he would dedicate himself to the propagation of the Buddhist faith in India. At present he was writing a book explaining the tenets of Buddhism in simple language for the benefit of the common man. It might take him a year to complete the work, but when it was finished he would embrace Buddhism.

This was the first time Ambedkar had actually declared that he would embrace Buddhism, as distinct from declaring that he was on his way to embracing it, and the first time that he had given anything like a definite date for that much-heralded event. But now, twenty years after the Yeola declaration had rocked Hindu India, the long journey from Hinduism to Buddhism was beginning to come to an end, and on his return to Bombay Ambedkar not only continued working on his book but started making arrangements for the holding of the actual conversion ceremony. He also started giving serious thought to the question of how one became a Buddhist, in the formal sense, and what becoming a Buddhist really meant. This was, in fact, the principal subject of the discussion I had with him four days after his Dehu Road speech, as well as the subject of the lecture which, at his request, I delivered to 3,000 of his followers on New Year's Day 1956. The question of how one became a Buddhist was also, apparently, the subject of correspondence between Ambedkar and Devapriya Valisinha, the General Secretary of the Maha Bodhi Society. Ambedkar was particularly concerned that the conversion of the so-called laity to Buddhism should be a real conversion, and that their membership of the Buddhist religion should not be merely nominal—as had been the case in India and was often the case in Buddhist countries at the present day. It was this concern that led him to publish, at about this time, his *Bauddha Puja Path* or 'Buddhist Worship', a little anthology of devotional texts in Pali (with Marathi translation) which he had started compiling as early as 1950, shortly after his return from Ceylon. The booklet began with the Three Refuges and Five Precepts and ended with the Ratana Sutta or 'Jewel Discourse', and also included verses to be recited when offering flowers to the Buddha and three of the most important verses of the *Dhammapada*. In his preface Ambedkar wrote, 'Consequent on the |recent| spread of Buddhism, people have become anxious to know about Buddhism, its literature and where it was available. In this regard, there appears to be a great eagerness among the people in India. In some cases they appear to have gone beyond the limits of eagerness. They became mad to know the methods of worship in the Buddhist religion as distinct from its teachings. They demanded the literature about worship in the Buddhist religion. Owing to my physical indisposition, I could not meet their demands until now.'[28]

Years of physical indisposition had also delayed the completion of a much more important work, but by February 1956 the last chapters of *The Buddha and His Dhamma* had been written and on 15 March Ambedkar was able to write—or dictate—the preface. From this time onwards he and his followers travelled along the road to conversion with increasing rapidity, and incidents that show in which direction they were moving occurred more and more frequently. In May a talk by Ambedkar on 'Why I Like Buddhism' was broadcast by the BBC, London, and in the same month he gave the manuscript of *The Buddha and His Dhamma* to the press for printing. 24 May was the anniversary of the Buddha's attainment of Enlightenment and, according to the Sinhalese Buddhist calendar, the 2500th anniversary of his parinirvana or final passing away. On that day Ambedkar addressed a meeting in Nare Park, Bombay, and declared that he would embrace Buddhism in October. He also took the opportunity of making clear the difference between Hinduism and Buddhism. Hinduism believed in God and the (permanent unchanging) soul, whereas in Buddhism there was neither God nor soul. Similarly, Hinduism believed in the chaturvarnya and the caste system, whereas Buddhism had no place for them. He added that his book on Buddhism would be published soon, that he had closed all the breaches in the organization of Buddhism and would consolidate it so that the tide of Buddhism would never recede in India. The Communists should study Buddhism, so as to know how to remove the ills of humanity. It was the great leader's last speech in Bombay.

On 23 September Ambedkar issued a press note announcing that his conversion to Buddhism would take place on 14 October in Nagpur. U Chandramani of Kusinara was invited to initiate him into the religion. 'It is our great wish,' Ambedkar wrote to the seventy-nine-year-old Burmese Bhikkhu, 'that you should officiate at the ceremony. You being the oldest monk in India we think it would be appropriate to have the ceremony performed by you.'[29] He also wrote to Devapriya Valisinha expressing his desire that the Maha Bodhi Society should participate in the function. On the morning of 11 October he flew from Delhi to Nagpur accompanied by his wife and P. N. Rattu, his private secretary. On the evening of 13 October he gave two press conferences, among other things telling the assembled newsmen that his Buddhism would adhere to the tenets of the faith as preached by the Buddha himself, without involving his people in the differences which had arisen with regard to the Hinayana and Mahayana. His Buddhism would be a sort of neo-Buddhism or Navayana. At 9.15 the following morning he ascended the dais that had been erected at one end of the Diksha Bhumi or 'Initiation Ground', as the spot afterwards came to be called; fifteen minutes later he and his wife took the Three Refuges and Five Precepts from U Chandramani, and fifteen or twenty minutes after that Ambedkar himself administered the same Three Refuges and Five Precepts—together with twenty-two supporting vows of his own devising—to the 380,000 men, women, and children who had assembled there in response to his call. They had reached the end of their long journey. They had now not only renounced Hinduism but embraced Buddhism. In the words of one of the twenty-two vows, they felt that they were being reborn. No longer were they Untouchables. They were human beings. They were Buddhists. After centuries of separation, they had re-established contact with their spiritual roots and could start producing flowers.

5

The Search for Roots

The search for roots is one of the preoccupations of our time. The white American tries to find out from which part of England or Ireland his forefathers emigrated to the New World, and under what circumstances, while the black American tries to discover from which part of West Africa he was sold into slavery and shipped to the cotton plantations on the other side of the Atlantic. For much of his life Bhimrao Ramji Ambedkar was preoccupied with a similar quest, though in his case it was largely confined to books and did not take him beyond the confines of his own land. Moreover, what he as an Untouchable was engaged in was not so much a sentimental search for roots as a scientific investigation into origins—though it was an investigation that proved to be not without important religious implications. Who were the Untouchables, and why had they become Untouchables? Why did the Caste Hindus treat them in the inhuman fashion that had persisted right down to the present day and threatened to go on for ever unless something was done about it? Questions like these had tormented Ambedkar for many years, but it was not until 1938 that he was able to take time off from his work for the Depressed Classes and start committing the results of his investigations to paper. In March that year, when it seems there was speculation as to why Dr Ambedkar had been less conspicuous on public platforms of late and why he was not devoting as much time as usual to the work of the Bombay Legislative Assembly, there appeared in the *Bombay Chronicle* an article that showed that the rising untouchable leader had not been passing his time in idleness. 'VOLUME THAT WILL CREATE CONSTERNATION AMONG ORTHODOX AND ROUSE REFORMER', ran the headline, 'DR AMBEDKAR'S FORTHCOMING "MAGNUM OPUS" '.¹ The article went on to reveal that a well known British publishing house had commissioned Ambedkar to prepare a comprehensive work on the Depressed Classes which would trace the origin of Untouchability, the various stages through which it had passed in the course of history, and the nature of the effect it had had on Hindu society and on Indian social, political, and cultural life during all those centuries. The article also revealed that the work would consist of seven chapters, beginning with an autobiographical chapter describing the author's own experience of Untouchability. Other chapters would explain the social, religious, and philosophical background of Untouchability, show the various means by which the Caste Hindu ruling class had kept the Untouchables down, and demonstrate the British Government's failure to do anything substantial to eradicate the evil. There would also be a chapter on the work of the Christian missionaries, and a chapter on the activities of the social reformers, both ancient and modern, and how Hindu society had reacted to these activities. This last chapter would bring the story up to date with an analysis of the activities of Mahatma Gandhi and Pandit Nehru. Concluding its account, the article said that the work would cover well over 600 pages and that its exposure of the systematic manner in which art, literature, and philosophy—in fact the entire cultural system—had been harnessed to maintain the domination of the ruling class was such that its publication would be bound to create a first class sensation in Indian politics and consternation in the ranks of the orthodox.

To what extent this prediction would have been fulfilled we have no means of telling. The magnum opus was never completed, and we do not even know the name of the enterprising British publishing house that commissioned it. But though the work was never completed, Ambedkar remained deeply preoccupied with the various questions with which it was to deal, and in the course of the following decade published two important books which, though complete in themselves, covered much the same ground as certain chapters of the projected *hauptwerk*. These two books were *What Congress and Gandhi Have Done to the Untouchables* (1945), a well documented exposure of the Congress Party's claim to represent the Untouchables, and *The Untouchables* (1948), a pioneering exploration of who the Untouchables were and how they became Untouchables. The first corresponded to the latter part of the seventh and last chapter of the unfinished magnum opus, while the second corresponded to the second and perhaps the third chapters. Unpublished writings by Ambedkar that cover much the same ground as other parts of the unfinished magnum opus include *Revolution and Counter-revolution* (the revolution being that of the Buddha and the counter-revolution that of the Brahmins), which at the time of Ambedkar's death was complete except for a few chapters, and the unfinished *Riddles of Hinduism*.

Two years after the appearance of the *Bombay Chronicle's* article Ambedkar again took its representative into his confidence, as it would seem, and there appeared in the same newspaper a report that showed not only that the untouchable scholar-politician was preoccupied with the same questions as in 1938 but that he thought he had found the answer to at least one of them, that is, the question of the origin of Untouchability. This time the headline ran, 'DR AMBEDKAR SAYS UNTOUCHABILITY WAS PUNISHMENT FOR STICKING TO BUDDHISM. BRAHMINS' ADAPTABILITY. WHEN BUDDHA STOPPED ANIMAL SACRIFICES, COWS WERE SANCTIFIED BY THEM'.[2] These were, in fact, the main points of Ambedkar's 'novel theory', as the *Chronicle's* representative called it, and the 1,200-word report was little more than a summary of *The Untouchables*, which did not appear until five years later. The delay was due partly to the fact that for Ambedkar the forties were years of high political office, first as Labour Member in the Viceroy's Executive Council and then as Minister for Law in the Nehru Government, and partly to the fact that during this period he was busy with several other literary projects.

One of these projects was *Who Were the Shudras?* (1946), which was published one year after *What Congress and Gandhi Have Done to the Untouchables* and two years before *The Untouchables*. This work did not cover any of the ground covered by the unfinished magnum opus, and did on a lesser but still very substantial scale for the Shudras what that work was to have done for the Depressed Classes and what *The Untouchables* actually did do in a more concentrated fashion. In each case there was a problem to be solved. In the case of the Untouchables it was the problem of who they were and how they had become Untouchables. In the case of the Shudras it was the problem of who they were and how they had come to be the fourth Varna in the Indo-Aryan society. Until the fifth Varna of the Untouchables came into being the Shudras were in the eyes of the Hindus the lowest of the low. How was it that under the chaturvarnya system—the system of graded inequality—the Shudra was 'not only placed at the bottom of the gradation . . . but subjected to ignominies and disabilities so as to prevent him from rising above the condition fixed for him by law'?[3] According to Ambedkar, the Shudras were not a dark-skinned non-Aryan race that had been conquered and enslaved by the fair-skinned Aryan invaders in prehistoric times, as some Western scholars believed. Nor had they been Shudras from the very beginning, as the Brahmins maintained on the basis of the cosmogonic myth set forth in the famous Purusha Shukta of the *Rig Veda*—the myth that describes the Brahmin or priest as originating from the mouth of the Cosmic Man, the Rajanya (i.e. Kshatriya) or warrior from his arms, the Vaishya or trader from his thighs, and the Shudra or menial from his feet. The truth was that the Shudras were Aryans, being one of the Aryan communities of the 'solar line', and thus belonged to the same race as the three other Varnas or classes. They did not form a separate Varna (originally there were only three Varnas) but ranked as part of the Kshatriya Varna or warrior class. In the course of the continuous violent conflict that took place between the Shudra kings and the Brahmins the latter were subjected to many tyrannies and indignities. As a result of this, they conceived a great hatred for the Shudras and out of this hatred refused to perform the upanayana ceremony for members of the Shudra community, that is, refused to perform for them the time honoured ceremony of initiation into full membership of Indo-Aryan society. Deprived of the upanayana, which only the Brahmins had the right to perform, 'the Shudras who were Kshatriyas became socially degraded, fell below the rank of the *Vaishyas* and thus came to be the fourth *Varna*.'[4]

Such were the terms in which Ambedkar himself summarized his answers to the twin questions of who were the Shudras and how they came to be the fourth Varna of the Indo-Aryan society. But no summary can do justice to the skill with which he organized his material (most of it drawn from the ancient Brahminical literature), to the closeness and cogency of his reasoning, or to the sleuth-like persistence with which he pursued his enquiry until, one clue having led to another, the problem he had set himself was eventually solved. *Who Were the Shudras?* does, in fact, read very much like a detective story or a murder mystery, and could well be described as a sociological whodunit. There is, so to speak, a dead body, in the form of the Shudras in their traditional state of degradation as described by Ambedkar in the third chapter of the book, entitled 'The Brahmanic Theory of the Status of the Shudra'. Who is responsible for the crime? How was it carried out? And is the victim really dead or only so badly injured as to appear dead?[5] These are the questions confronting the sociological detective, and Ambedkar brings to bear on them a combination of scholarship, logic, and a determination to get at the truth despite threats from interested parties that, in the end, enables him to track down the criminal and find out exactly how he committed his crime and for what reason.

The Untouchables, which Ambedkar described as a sequel to *Who Were the Shudras?,* also reads like a sociological whodunit. This time there is an even more cruelly mutilated body, in the shape of the still worse state of degradation of the 50,000,000 Untouchables produced by Hindu civilization, and Ambedkar brings to the solution of this even darker mystery the same combination of qualities that is so conspicuous in the earlier book. In the case of *The Untouchables*, however, he has 'to use his imagination and intuition to bridge the gaps left in the chain of facts by links not yet discovered and to propound a working hypothesis suggesting how facts which cannot be connected by known facts might have been interconnected.'[6] Such a procedure is quite permissible. The origin of Untouchability is lost in antiquity, and the attempt to explain it is not the same as writing history from texts. It is a case of gathering survivals of the past, placing them together, and making them tell the story of their birth. One's task is analogous to that of an archaeologist who reconstructs a city from broken stones, of a palaeontologist who conceives a new animal from scattered bones and teeth, or of a painter who reads the lines of the horizon and the smallest vestiges on the slopes of the hill to make up a scene. 'In this sense the book is a work of art even more than of history. The origin of Untouchability lies buried in a dead past which nobody knows. To make it alive is like an attempt to reclaim to history a city which has been dead since ages past and present it as it was in its original condition.'[7]

In setting out to clear up the mystery of who the Untouchables were and how they came to be Untouchables Ambedkar is very conscious of the fact that there is, so to speak, a dead body (corresponding to the buried city of his own analogy). He is very conscious that a crime has been committed. But he is no less conscious of the fact that nobody else is aware that there is a dead body in the house and that it is important to find out who is responsible. The reason nobody else notices that there is a dead body in the house of Hindu civilization (in fact, three dead bodies, if one includes the Criminal Tribes and the Aboriginal Tribes) is that for the orthodox Hindu the observance of Untouchability is a normal and natural thing and as such calls for neither expiation nor explanation. For Ambedkar, however, Untouchability is by no means either a normal or a natural thing and he is, therefore, very conscious of the fact that there is a dead body and that a crime has been committed. He is also very conscious of the fact that this crime is unique for, as he proceeds to show in the first two chapters of the book, Untouchability among Hindus is a very different thing from Untouchability among non-Hindus. Untouchability is based on the notion of pollution or defilement, and pollution can be caused by the occurrence of certain events (for example death), by contact with certain things, and by contact with certain persons, just as it can be removed with the help of certain purificatory agents and purificatory ceremonies. So far there is little difference between the notion of pollution obtaining in primitive societies like those of the Polynesians and East Africans, or in ancient societies like those of the Egyptians, Greeks, and Romans, on the one hand, and the notion of pollution prevalent among the Hindus on the other. Among Hindus, however, there is another form of Untouchability: the hereditary Untouchability of 429 different communities amounting to 50—60,000,000 people. These people are held to be impure, and contact with them polluting, not because of anything they have done in their individual capacity but simply because they have been born into a certain caste. Moreover, their impurity is not temporary but permanent, and instead of being isolated for a limited period they are permanently segregated in separate quarters. What is the reason for the existence of this unique form of Untouchability among Hindus? In particular, why do the Untouchables live outside the village and what made their Untouchability permanent and ineradicable? The remaining chapters of the book are devoted to finding the answers to these two questions.

Ambedkar begins by pointing out that there are only two possibilities. Either the Untouchables originally lived in the village together with the Caste Hindus and were subsequently declared Untouchables and made to live outside it, or else they lived outside the village from the very beginning. Of these two possibilities he finds the second more acceptable, since the phenomenon under discussion is not confined to a single village or area but exists all over India and it is inconceivable that at some time in the past all the Untouchables in the country should have been transplanted from within the village to outside the village. The Untouchables therefore must have lived outside the village from the very beginning. Here too there are only two possibilities. Either the Untouchables lived outside the village from the very beginning and also were Untouchables from the very beginning, or else they lived outside the village even before they became Untouchables and continued to live outside it because of the supervention of Untouchability at a later stage. Ambedkar believes that only the latter possibility is worth consideration. But this raises a very difficult question. Why did the (future) Untouchables live outside the village? What forced them to do so?

In order to answer this further question Ambedkar invokes the help of sociology, explaining that it is necessary to bear in mind that modern society differs from primitive society in two respects. Firstly, primitive society consisted of nomadic communities while modern society consists of settled communities; secondly, primitive society consisted of tribal communities based on blood relationship whereas modern society consists of local communities based on territorial affiliation. Thus in the transformation of primitive society into modern society there are two lines of evolution, one leading from the nomadic community to the settled community, the other leading from the tribal community to the territorial community. Confining the enquiry to the first line of evolution, one has to understand what made primitive society nomadic and what happened in the course of the transition from nomadic to settled life. Primitive society was nomadic, in the sense of migratory, because its wealth was in cattle and its cattle needed fresh pastures. It became fixed in one spot, or in other words became a settled community, only when its wealth changed from cattle to land and this happened when man discovered the art of agriculture. For an understanding of what happened in the course of the transition from nomadic life to settled life, one has to bear in mind two facts. Firstly, all the tribes did not become fixed in one spot at one and the same time: some became settled and some remained nomadic. Secondly, in their nomadic state the tribes were always at war with one another. When some tribes became settled the tribes that remained nomadic soon found that organizing raids on the wealthy and comparatively defenceless settled tribes was a more profitable business than fighting one another. This created a problem for the settled tribes. Fortunately for them, however, the constant warfare between the nomadic tribes had brought into existence a third group of people. These were the Broken Men, as sociologists call them, or the scattered remnants of defeated tribes, who, unable to join another tribe (for tribal organization was based on community of blood), lived in constant danger of attack. Thus the Broken Men needed shelter and protection no less than the settled tribes needed a body of men to keep watch and ward against the raids of the nomadic tribes. In the end a bargain was struck between the two groups. The Broken Men agreed to do the work of watch and ward for the settled tribes, and in return the settled tribes agreed to give the Broken Men food and shelter. Only one thing remained to be decided. Where were the Broken Men to stay? They could not stay in the midst of the settled community because according to primitive notions only persons of the same tribe, i.e. the same blood, could live together, and the Broken Men were aliens. For this reason, and because it was in any case desirable that they should be in a position to meet the raids of any hostile nomadic tribe, the Broken Men were assigned quarters outside the village.

Having cleared the ground by explaining what made primitive society nomadic and what happened in the course of the transition from nomadic life to settled life, Ambedkar returns to the main question, namely, why do the Untouchables live outside the village? According to him, the Untouchables were originally only Broken Men and it was because they were originally only Broken Men that they lived outside the village. As Hindu society passed from nomadic life to the life of the settled village community, the same process must have taken place in India as took place elsewhere. In primitive Hindu society there must have been both settled tribes and Broken Men. It is therefore natural to suppose that, since the (future) Untouchables were originally only Broken Men they lived outside the village from the very beginning and that Untouchability had nothing to do with the matter.

Ambedkar is, of course, conscious that his theory is a novel one and that he will be asked to produce evidence in its support. Direct evidence, he admits, has yet to be collected, but there are two pointers on account of which it can be said that the

Untouchables were Broken Men. The first of these pointers is the fact that the name Antya and its derivatives was given to certain communities by the ancient Hindu law books. Orthodox Hindu scholarship maintains that Antya means '(born) last' or '(born) at the end' and that since, in the order of creation, the Untouchable was born last, Antya means an Untouchable. Ambedkar points out that this explanation contradicts the Vedic theory of creation, according to which it was the Shudra who was born last, the Untouchable not being mentioned at all. In his view the word antya means not '(born) at the end' of creation but '(born) at the end' of the village and dates from the time when some people lived inside the village while others lived outside it. Those who lived outside the village must have done so because they were Broken Men. The second pointer on account of which it can be said that the Untouchables were Broken Men is the position occupied by the Mahars—the single largest untouchable community in Maharashtra—in relation to the Caste Hindus. It is noteworthy that Mahars are to be found in every village, that every village in Maharashtra is surrounded by a wall and that the Mahars have their quarters outside the wall, that the Mahars keep watch and ward on behalf of the village, and that the Mahars claim no less than fifty-two rights against the Caste Hindus, the most important of them being the right to collect food from the villagers, the right to collect corn from them in harvest time, and the right to appropriate their dead domestic animals. If the case of the Mahars is typical of Untouchables throughout India (and Ambedkar admits that the matter awaits investigation) then it follows that, in his own words, 'there was a stage in the history of India when Broken Men belonging to other tribes came to the settled tribes and made a bargain whereby the Broken Men were allowed to settle on the border of the village, were required to do certain duties, and in return were to be given certain rights.'[8]

Thus there is some evidence in support of Ambedkar's theory that the Untouchables were originally only Broken Men and that it was because they were only Broken Men that they lived outside the village. This evidence would be stronger if there were any other cases known to history of Broken Men living outside the village, and if it could be shown that what was said to have occurred in India had actually occurred elsewhere. Fortunately Ambedkar is able to cite the parallel cases of the Fuidhirs or 'Stranger-tenants' of ancient Ireland, as revealed in the Brehon Laws as summarized by Sir Henry Maine, and of the Alltudes or 'Unfree-tenants' of ancient Wales, as described by Mr Seebhom in his account of the organization of the Welsh village in primitive times. Both the Fuidhirs and the Alltudes were made to live outside the village and both were made to live outside it for the same reason, namely, that they belonged to different tribes and were of different blood. Thus the case of the Untouchables was not the only case of a people living outside the village. Indeed, it illustrated a phenomenon that was universal and marked by the same distinctive features everywhere.

There was however one important respect in which the case of the Untouchables differed from that of the Broken Men in other parts of the world. In other parts of the world the separate quarters of the Broken Men eventually disappeared and, as common territory rather than common blood became the bond of union, the Broken Men themselves became part of the settled tribe and were absorbed into it. The only place where this development did not occur was India, and according to Ambedkar the reason it did not occur in India was that here the notion of Untouchability supervened and perpetuated the difference between kindred and non-kindred, tribesmen and non-tribesmen, in another form, namely, in the form of the difference between Touchable and Untouchable. But why did this new factor enter into the situation? *What was the origin of Untouchability?* With this crucial question we come to the very heart of the book, and to the point where Ambedkar's scientific investigation into origins starts becoming indistinguishable from a spiritual search for roots. Before giving his own answer to the question, however, Ambedkar considers two earlier theories of the origin of Untouchability. According to the first theory the origin of Untouchability is racial, the Untouchables being non-Aryan, non-Dravidian aboriginals who had been conquered and subjugated by the Dravidians. According to the second theory the origin of Untouchability is occupational, being found in the filthy and unclean nature of the occupations in which the Untouchables engaged. Ambedkar has no difficulty in disproving both these theories. In the case of the first he shows, on anthropometric and ethnological grounds, that the Aryans, the Dravidians, and the allegedly aboriginal Untouchables all belonged to the same race. In the course of the second he shows that under certain circumstances Brahmins, Kshatriyas, Vaishyas, and Shudras alike could engage in even the filthiest of occupations without thereby becoming Untouchables. The earlier theories having been disproved in this manner the way is now clear for Ambedkar to put forward his own theory of the origin of Untouchability.

He begins by drawing attention to the Census Reports. Since 1910 these had divided the Hindus into three categories: Hindus, Animists and Tribals, and Depressed Classes or Untouchables. The division was made in accordance with ten criteria, out of which the first five served to differentiate the Hindus from the Animists and Tribals and the second five to divide the Hindus from the Untouchables. The replies received by the Census Commissioner to questions based on the second five criteria revealed that the Untouchables did not receive mantra-initiation from a Brahmin; that they were not served by good Brahmins as family priests; that they had, in fact, no Brahmin priests at all; and that they ate beef and did not reverence the cow. These facts were important, especially the fact that the Untouchables had no Brahmin priests, for they showed that the Brahmins shunned the Untouchables. Owing to the onesidedness of the questions put by the Census Commissioner, however, what the replies did not reveal was that the Untouchables also shunned the Brahmins. If the Untouchables did not have Brahmin priests, and instead had priests drawn from their own community, this was not only because the Brahmins refused to be employed as priests by the Untouchables; it was also because the Untouchables were reluctant to employ them as priests. Surprising though it may seem, in much the same way that the Brahmins regarded the Untouchables as impure and inauspicious the Untouchables regarded the Brahmins as impure and inauspicious—a fact for which there was ample evidence. The reason for this strange state of affairs, Ambedkar says, is more important than the state of affairs itself, for behind it is hidden the clue to the origin of Untouchability. This clue consists in the fact that the mutual antipathy that existed between the Brahmins and the Untouchables can be explained only on the basis of the hypothesis that the Broken Men (as the Untouchables originally were) were Buddhists. Because they were Buddhists they did not revere the Brahmins, did not employ them as their priests, and regarded them as impure, and because the Broken Men were Buddhists the Brahmins, for their part, preached hatred and contempt against them with the result that the Broken Men came to be regarded as Untouchables.

Ambedkar is well aware that there is no direct evidence for his hypothesis that the Broken Men were Buddhists, but in his opinion no evidence is necessary. The majority of Hindus, he declares, were Buddhists (in this connection he appears to be using the term Hindu in its American sense of 'Indian') and we may take it that the Broken Men were Buddhists too. But though there is no direct evidence that the Broken Men were Buddhists, there is certainly evidence that there existed hatred and abhorrence against the Buddhists in the minds of the Hindus and that this feeling was created by the Brahmins. (Though Ambedkar does not mention the fact, the reason the Brahmins as a class were so hostile to Buddhism was that its critique of the notion of hereditary superiority had the effect of undermining their privileged position in society.) How widespread the spirit of hatred and contempt against the followers of the Buddha had become can be observed, Ambedkar points out, from certain scenes of classical Sanskrit drama. In the well known *Mrichchhakatika* or 'Little Clay Cart', for instance, an inoffensive Buddhist monk is not only avoided as inauspicious by the hero of the play but also abused and beaten by one of the other characters. Even in the absence of any direct evidence for his hypothesis, therefore, Ambedkar has no difficulty in believing that the Broken Men were Buddhists who, when Brahmanism triumphed over Buddhism, did not return to it as easily as others did. If we accept this, he says, we can see why the Untouchables shunned the Brahmins. We can also see why the Broken Men

93

came to be regarded as Untouchables. 'The Broken Men hated the Brahmins because the Brahmins were the enemies of Buddhism and the Brahmins imposed Untouchability upon the Broken Men because they would not leave Buddhism. On this reasoning it is possible to conclude that one of the roots of Untouchability lies in the hatred and contempt which the Brahmins created against those who were Buddhist.'[9] In the blunt words of the *Bombay Chronicle's* headline ten years earlier Untouchability was a punishment for sticking to Buddhism.

Awareness that India had once been a Buddhist country, and that many of their own ancestors must have been Buddhists, had, of course, been growing among educated Indians for some time. Ambedkar fully shared this awareness. Indeed, he shared it to a greater degree than any of his contemporaries. For him Buddhism was not just an object of archaeological interest, much less still an excuse for indulgence in chauvinistic self-congratulation. For him—especially after the Yeola declaration—Buddhism represented a spiritual possibility, even a religious alternative, and though it was an alternative which he did not, at first, consider as seriously as Sikhism, it was the one for which he eventually opted and towards which, by the time *The Untouchables* was published, he was already moving. To what extent his decision in favour of Buddhism was influenced by the fact that the Untouchables were originally Buddhists, and Untouchability itself a punishment for sticking to Buddhism, it is difficult to say. At the very least, his discovery of the hidden connection between the Untouchables and Buddhism must have enabled him, as an Untouchable himself, to identify with Buddhism in a way that he had not done before and to feel that, in embracing Buddhism, he and his followers would not be converting to a new religion so much as returning to the old one. In other words, Ambedkar's discovery that the Untouchables were originally Buddhists represented a discovery of his own spiritual roots, and the fact that those roots were Buddhist roots must have made it easier for him to establish an emotional as well as an intellectual connection with Buddhism than would otherwise have been the case. It is even possible that, without that emotional connection, he may not have been able to take the final step and actually go for Refuge to the Buddha, Dharma, and Sangha.

Be that as it may, though Ambedkar has shown that the Untouchables were originally Buddhists, and that they became Untouchables because they stuck to Buddhism, he has yet to show why only the Broken Men (as the Untouchables then were) became Untouchables. After all, the hatred and contempt preached by the Brahmins was directed against Buddhists in general and not against the Broken Men in particular. What, then, was the additional circumstance on account of which Untouchability was imposed on the Broken Men? In order to answer this question and thus complete his solution of the mystery of Untouchability by showing not only why but how it originated, Ambedkar refers to the fifth and last of the five criteria in accordance with which the Census Reports from 1910 onwards had divided the Hindus from the Untouchables. The criterion related to beef-eating, and Ambedkar has no hesitation in affirming that the Broken Men came to be treated as Untouchables because they ate beef. In the first place, only the Untouchables eat dead cows and it is *only* those who eat dead cows who are tainted with Untouchability. In the second place, even those Hindus who are non-vegetarians never eat cow's flesh, with the result that the Touchables, who are united in their objection to the eating of cow's flesh, are completely marked off from the Untouchables, who eat it without compunction and as a matter of course. It is therefore not too far-fetched to suggest that those who are nauseated by beef-eating should treat those who eat beef as Untouchables.

Not that speculation as to whether beef-eating was or was not the principal reason for the rise of Untouchability is really necessary. Ambedkar has no difficulty in showing that the authors of the ancient Hindu law books knew very well that the origin of Untouchability was to be found in the eating of beef. He therefore concludes that his new approach to the origin of Untouchability has revealed that the latter had two sources, one being the general atmosphere of scorn and contempt spread by the Brahmins against those who were Buddhists and the other the habit of beef-eating kept on by the Broken Men. The first of these circumstances alone, he believes, cannot account for the stigma of Untouchability attaching itself to the Broken Men, for the scorn and contempt for Buddhists that was spread by the Brahmins was of a general kind and affected all Buddhists, not only the Broken Men. 'The reason why the Broken Men only became Untouchables was because in addition to being Buddhists they retained their habit of beef-eating which gave additional ground for offence to the Brahmins to carry their new-found love and reverence to the cow to its logical conclusion. We may therefore conclude that though the Broken Men were exposed to scorn and contempt on the ground that they were Buddhist the main cause of their Untouchability was beef-eating.'[10]

The theory that beef-eating was the cause of Untouchability naturally gives rise to a number of questions, and Ambedkar is well aware that unless these questions are answered the theory will remain 'under a cloud' and that it will be regarded as plausible but may not be accepted as conclusive. He therefore devotes the remaining chapters of *The Untouchables* not just to dealing with the questions which, he says, critics are sure to ask, but to dealing with them in such a way as to demonstrate the exact nature of the process whereby beef-eating came to be the cause of Untouchability. Thus he shows that, contrary to popular belief, there was a time when Hindus—both Brahmins and non-Brahmins—ate not only flesh but also beef; that the non-Brahmins gave up beef-eating (though not necessarily the eating of meat) in imitation of the Brahmins, and that the Brahmins themselves gave up beef-eating and started worshipping the cow as part of their strategy for establishing the supremacy of Brahmanism over Buddhism. Here Ambedkar points out that the strife between Buddhism and Brahmanism is a crucial fact of Indian history, and that unless this is realized it is impossible to explain some of the features of Hinduism. Since the struggle in which the two creeds were engaged lasted for 400 years, and left indelible marks on the religion, society, and politics of India, the present book is not the place for describing the full story of the struggle. All he can do is to mention a few salient points.

The most important of the points mentioned by Ambedkar is

the fact that Buddhism had taken such a strong hold on the minds of the masses that, in order to regain their lost power and prestige, the Brahmins had no alternative but to adopt certain features of Buddhism. Thus the Buddhists having set up images of the Buddha and built stupas the Brahmins, in their turn, built temples and installed in them the images of Hindu gods—all with the object of drawing people away from the worship of the Buddha. Similarly, the Buddhists having rejected the Brahmanical religion, which consisted of Yajna or animal sacrifice, particularly sacrifice of the cow, the Brahmins sought to improve their position by abandoning Yajna as a form of worship. What was more, they not only gave up the eating of beef, of which they were notoriously fond, but actually became vegetarian, the reason for this being 'that without becoming vegetarian the Brahmins could not have recovered the ground they had lost to their rival, namely, Buddhism. In this connection [Ambedkar continues] it must be remembered that there was one respect in which Brahmanism suffered in public esteem as compared to Buddhism. That was the practice of animal sacrifice which was the essence of Brahmanism and to which Buddhism was deadly opposed. That in an agricultural population there should be respect for Buddhism and revulsion against Brahmanism which involved slaughter of animals including cows and bullocks is only natural. What could the Brahmins do to recover the lost ground? To go one better than the Buddhist Bhikshus—not only to give up meat-eating [i.e. beef-eating] but to become vegetarians—which they did.'[11]

The reason Ambedkar speaks of the Brahmins as going one better than the Bhikshus and giving up meat-eating and becoming vegetarians is that, as he proceeds to show, the Bhikshus were permitted to eat meat that was 'pure' in the sense of being from an animal the slaughter of which had not been seen or heard or suspected by them as having been on their account. It is worth noting, however, that the Bhikshus were not all agreed in thinking that the eating of 'pure' meat was permitted to them and that the permission had come from the Buddha himself. Those Bhikshus who were Mahayanists (that is, who studied the Mahayana sutras and worshipped the

Bodhisattvas) certainly did not think that 'pure' meat was permitted to them, and there is some evidence that those who belonged to the prominent and influential Sarvastivada school did not think so either. In becoming vegetarians, therefore, the Brahmins went one better than some Buddhist Bhikshus but not better than all. Not that this really affects the main thrust of Ambedkar's argument, for if, in becoming vegetarians, the Brahmins only went one better than some Bhikshus they undoubtedly went one better than all Bhikshus—indeed, than all Buddhists—in making the cow a sacred animal and inducing the Gupta kings to treat cow-slaughter as a capital offence.

Having demonstrated the exact nature of the process whereby beef-eating came to be the cause of Untouchability, thus showing the convincingness of his theory, Ambedkar has only to explain why, when the non-Brahmins gave up beef-eating in imitation of the Brahmins, the Broken men did not do likewise. The reason was twofold. 'In the first place, imitation was too costly. They could not afford it. The flesh of the dead cow was their principal sustenance. Without it they would starve. In the second place, carrying [away] the dead cow had become an obligation though originally it was a privilege. As they could not escape carrying [away] the dead cow they did not mind using the flesh as food in the manner in which they were doing previously.'[12] Thus the Broken Men, who in any case were exposed to scorn and contempt on the ground that they were Buddhist, continued to eat beef when everyone else had given it up, and because they ate beef—as well as because they stuck to Buddhism—they were treated as Untouchables. This did not, of course, happen all at once, and it is therefore not possible to fix an exact date when the seed of Untouchability could be said to have been sown. But it is possible to give an approximate date. Since the root of Untouchability is beef-eating, it follows that the date of the birth of Untouchability must be intimately connected with the ban on cow-slaughter and on eating beef. Cow-slaughter was made a capital offence by the Gupta kings in the 4th century. 'We can, therefore, say with some confidence that Untouchability was born some time about 400 AD. It is born out of the struggle between Buddhism and Brahmanism which has completely moulded the history of India and the study of which is so woefully neglected by students of Indian history.'[13]

With these sombre words the book concludes. Ambedkar has solved the mystery of who the Untouchables were and how they became Untouchables. He has discovered his own spiritual roots and, in this way, established an emotional as well as an intellectual connection with Buddhism—a connection without which he may not have been able to go for Refuge to the Buddha, Dharma, and Sangha. But the fact that Ambedkar had established an emotional connection with Buddhism certainly did not mean that he had stopped thinking about it. He was thinking about it more vigorously than ever, and his thought was to be of significance not only to his own followers but to Buddhists throughout the world.

6

Thinking about Buddhism

Between the publication of *The Untouchables* and the organizing of the Nagpur conversion ceremony there elapsed eight years. Surveying this crucial period of Ambedkar's life one cannot help wishing that there had been someone at hand to perform for him the service that Boswell performed for Johnson (whom Ambedkar resembled in a number of respects) and that H. N. Coleridge performed for Coleridge (whom Ambedkar did not resemble at all), for we should then have possessed a record of Ambedkar's table-talk, and if we had possessed a record of his table-talk we would have been in a better position to follow his thinking at the time—especially his thinking about Buddhism. As things are, we have to rely for our knowledge of his thoughts on this subject mainly on the glimpses of them that he gives us in his speeches in and out of Parliament, in newspaper interviews, in letters, and in his published writings. Of these the writings are naturally the most important, though they are by no means as extensive as one might wish and show the nature of Ambedkar's thoughts on Buddhism only to a limited degree. Leaving aside the polemical article entitled 'The Rise And Fall of the Hindu Woman. Who was Responsible for It?', which in the present context is only of peripheral interest, we find that Ambedkar's thoughts on Buddhism are contained in his article on 'The Buddha and the Future of His Religion' and in certain sections of *The Buddha and His Dhamma*. Since the latter was not published until nearly a year after Ambedkar's death, and since these sections will in any case fall to be considered when the book is dealt with as a whole, this leaves us with 'The Buddha and the Future of His Religion' as the principal evidence for the way in which Ambedkar was thinking about Buddhism during the years immediately preceding his conversion.

The article appeared in the April—May 1950 issue of the *Maha Bodhi*. This was not without significance. Founded by Anagarika Dharmapala in 1892 as the official organ of the Maha Bodhi Society, the *Maha Bodhi* was at that time the leading English-language Buddhist magazine and enjoyed an extensive, even if numerically small, circulation among English-speaking Buddhists throughout the world. On account of its president being a Bengali Brahmin the Society itself was anathema to Ambedkar (as I was to discover on the occasion of our first meeting), and he therefore must have allowed 'The Buddha and the Future of His Religion' to appear in the pages of the *Maha Bodhi* only because he wanted to share his thoughts on Buddhism with Buddhists outside India and, in fact, with students of religion and philosophy everywhere. Moreover, the April-May issue of the *Maha Bodhi* was always a Vaishakha number, that is, a special double issue in commemoration of the Buddha's attainment of Enlightenment, and reached more people than any other issue of the magazine.

But though 'The Buddha and the Future of His Religion' made its appearance in the *Maha Bodhi* it bore very little resemblance to the dry, academic disquisitions on Buddhist history and doctrine by scholarly Hindus, or the pompous pronouncements by Buddhist dignitaries, that the magazine only too often featured. Ambedkar's 6,500-word article was the work of a man who was in deadly earnest. It was the work of a man who was as yet only 'on his way to embrace Buddhism' and who knew that, when he did finally take that momentous step, it would bring about a radical change in the lives of millions of his fellow countrymen and alter, perhaps, the entire course of Indian history. It was the work of a man who was not afraid to think for himself and who was not afraid to say what he thought. At the same time, the article was the work of a man who was in a hurry and had no time to revise and polish. From a literary point of view 'The Buddha and the Future of His Religion' is therefore distinctly rough in texture, reminding one of a stream of lava that, issuing white-hot from the depths of a volcano, has set in bold and jagged shapes, or of a lump of gold that has come from the furnace with fragments of rock still adhering to it and which has yet to be wrought into ornaments.

The fact that 'The Buddha and the Future of His Religion' is rough in texture does not however mean that Ambedkar's thinking about Buddhism is not fully defined or that the article itself is unsystematic. Though short, the article is in fact divided into five numbered sections, each with its own distinctive subject-matter. In the first section Ambedkar shows what distinguishes the Buddha from the founders of three other major religions; in the second—which is the longest section—he compares Buddhism with Hinduism; in the third he expresses his faith in the revival of Buddhism in India; in the fourth he summarizes his conclusions with regard to how Buddhism stands in comparison with other, non-Hindu religions, and in the fifth he outlines the three steps that have to be taken if the ideal of spreading Buddhism is to be realized. Thus in the course of some sixteen pages a great deal of ground is covered, and Ambedkar manages to make a number of points of enormous significance and value. At the same time, he makes them in so condensed a manner that, as with the aphorisms in which the sages of old summarized their knowledge of the different arts and sciences, a certain amount of commentary is needed if their meaning is to be fully appreciated.

This is very much the case with the first section of the article, where Ambedkar boldly declares that what distinguishes the Buddha from Jesus, Mahommed, and Krishna—the founders of the three other major religions—is his self-abnegation. By the Buddha's self-abnegation Ambedkar means his refusal to claim for himself the kind of position that Jesus, Mahommed, and Krishna claimed for themselves, and it is not without significance that in enumerating these three founders he should enumerate them in the order of the increasing largeness of their claims, and, therefore, in the order of their increasing distance from the Buddha. Thus throughout the Bible (that is, throughout the Four Gospels) Jesus insists that he is the son of God and that those who wish to enter the kingdom of God will fail to do so if they do not recognize him as such. Mahommed went a step further. Like Jesus he claimed that he was a messenger of God on earth (here Ambedkar is apparently treating Jesus's claim to be the son of God as equivalent to his claim to be the messenger of God), but he further insisted that he was the last messenger. On this footing he declared that those who wanted salvation must not only accept that he was a messenger of God but also accept that he was the last messenger. Krishna went a step beyond both Jesus and Mahommed, refusing to be satisfied with being merely the son or the messenger of God, or even with being the last messenger of God. According to Ambedkar, Krishna was not even satisfied with calling himself God. 'He claimed that he was *Parameshwar* [or 'God Supreme'] or as his followers described him *Devadhideva*, God of Gods'.[1] In representing Krishna as claiming to be Parameshwar Ambedkar is regarding him, for the purpose of his article, as a historical figure and regarding that figure as having actually made that claim—a claim that the *Bhagavad-gita* or 'Song Celestial' and other Hindu scriptures do in fact represent him as making. There is no doubt, however, that Ambedkar was well aware that for the majority of Western scholars the blue-complexioned charioteer of Arjuna and lover of the Gopis belongs to Hindu myth and legend and that he can be regarded as the founder of Hinduism only in a strictly symbolic sense.

Having described the claims made by Jesus, Mahommed, and Krishna, Ambedkar proceeds to emphasize the very different attitude assumed by the Buddha who, he says, never arrogated to himself any such status as they did. In striking contrast to all three of them, 'He was born a son of man and was content to remain a common man and preached his gospel as a common man. He never claimed any supernatural origin or supernatural powers nor did he perform miracles to prove his supernatural powers.'[2] In speaking of the Buddha as a common man Ambedkar does not, of course, mean to deny that there is any difference between the Buddha and ordinary humanity. The Buddha is, after all, the Enlightened One, and between the Enlightened One and those who are not Enlightened Ones—who are not even Stream-Entrants—the difference is so great as to be virtually unimaginable. What Ambedkar is really saying, therefore, is that the difference between the Buddha and ordinary humanity consists not in the fact that the Buddha occupies an inherently privileged position or status, so to speak, but rather in the fact that he has attained a higher level of spiritual development. No one can be the son and messenger of God in the sense that Jesus was, or the last messenger of God in the sense that Mahommed was, and certainly no one can be Parameshwar or 'God Supreme' as Krishna was, for there is by definition only one son of God, one last messenger of God, one Parameshwar. But anyone can become a Buddha, that is, anyone who makes the effort that the Buddha made and attains the level of spiritual development that the Buddha attained, and it is for this reason the Ambedkar speaks of the Buddha as a common man. The Buddha is a common man in the sense that he has achieved nothing that a common man (that is, one born a common man) cannot achieve likewise. Similarly, in saying that the Buddha 'never claimed any supernatural origin or supernatural powers nor did he perform miracles to prove his supernatural powers' Ambedkar does not mean to deny the difference between supernatural powers, such as those possessed by Jesus by virtue of his status as the son and messenger of God, and supernormal powers, such as those acquired by the Buddha in the course of his experience of concentration and meditation. Supernormal powers are extensions of ordinary human faculties and can be acquired by anyone who practises the necessary disciplines. They do not constitute evidence for the attainment of wisdom or insight—and it is wisdom or insight alone that leads to Enlightenment.

Because the Buddha never claimed any supernatural origin or

supernatural powers for himself it naturally followed that he never claimed any supernatural sanction, or divine authority, for his teaching, in the way that Jesus, Mahommed, and Krishna did. All he claimed for it was that it was a reasonable teaching, and that it was possible for a sincere and open-minded person to experience the truth of it for himself, in this very existence. In Ambedkar's words, the Buddha 'preached his gospel as a common man', that is, he preached it not as something thundered by God in the ears of a reluctant humanity but simply as something communicated by a man to his fellow men—by a man who was an Enlightened One to men who were not, as yet, Enlightened Ones—and which the latter were free to accept or reject as they saw fit. The Buddha did not issue orders, but only advised, encouraged, and inspired. He did not pick men up and carry them bodily to the goal of the spiritual life, as it were, but only showed them the way by which they could reach it on their own two feet. Ambedkar is therefore able to say, 'The Buddha made a clear distinction between Margadata |or Giver of the Way| and Mokshadata |or Giver of Salvation|. Jesus, Mahommed, and Krishna claimed for themselves the role of *Mokshadata*. The Buddha was satisfied with playing the role of *Margadata*.'[3] To this one can only add that the Buddha was not satisfied with the role of Margadata in the sense of being content with an inferior role, for according to Buddhism there is in fact no such role as that of Mokshadata and to think so is a delusion.

Besides being distinguished from the three other founders of religions by his self-abnegation the Buddha is distinguished from them by the fact that he did not claim infallibility for his teaching. This was the natural consequence of his preaching his gospel 'as a common man', for infallibility can be claimed only for the word of God and for it to be the word of God a teaching must come either from a messenger of God, as in the case of Jesus and Mahommed, or directly from God himself, as in the case of Krishna, and the Buddha claimed to be neither God nor a messenger of God. Nor is that all. From the fact that the Buddha did not claim infallibility for his teaching there follow certain consequences of great practical significance—consequences which Ambedkar is not afraid to draw. 'In the *Mahaparinibbana*

Sutta,' he says, '[the Buddha] told Ananda that his religion was based on reason and experience and that his followers should not accept his teaching as correct and binding merely because it emanated from him. Being based on reason and experience they were free to modify or even abandon any of his teachings if it was found that at a given time and in given circumstances they did not apply.'[4] In other words, that which is not infallible is capable of revision. The passage of the *Mahaparinibbana Sutta* or 'Book of the Great Decease' to which Ambedkar refers is probably the well known one where the Buddha, on the eve of his departure from the world, tells his faithful attendant, 'When I am gone, Ananda, let the Order, if it should so wish, abolish all the lesser and minor precepts.'[5] As it happened, the Order did not so wish. On considering the matter shortly after the Buddha's death, they declined to avail themselves of his permission, maintaining—according to tradition—that he had given it simply in order to test the Bhikkhus, 'to try whether, if leave were granted them, they would, after his death, revoke the lesser and minor regulations, or still adhere to them.'[6] To this Ambedkar would doubtless have replied that if there was any question of a test the Order had failed it, for obviously the Buddha 'wished his religion not to be encumbered with the dead wood of the past. He wanted that it should remain evergreen and serviceable at all times. That is why he gave liberty to his followers to chip and chop as the necessities of the case required.'[7] In drawing such a conclusion Ambedkar must have been aware that, nearly 2,500 years after the Buddha's death, Buddhism as practised in the Buddhist countries of Asia was by no means unencumbered with dead wood and that if it was to be made serviceable to him and his followers a good deal of chipping and chopping would have to be done. Not that Ambedkar saw such chipping and chopping as a negative thing. For him the fact that the Buddha had given liberty to his followers to 'chip and chop' was nothing less than a direct expression of his teaching and a triumphant affirmation of the nature of Buddhism as a religion based not on authority but on reason and experience. It demonstrated the Buddha's faith in his teaching and in his followers. Indeed, it demonstrated his courage—a courage that, Ambedkar believes, no other religious teacher had shown. 'They were afraid of permitting repair. For they felt that the liberty to repair may be used to demolish the structure they had reared. The Buddha had no such fear. He was sure that even the most violent iconoclast will not be able to destroy the core of his religion.'[8]

With this insight into the psychology of the founders of religion Ambedkar brings the first section of his article to a close. He has shown that what distinguishes the Buddha from Jesus, Mahommed, and Krishna is his self-abnegation and the fact that he did not claim infallibility for what he taught, as well as his courage in giving his followers the freedom to revise his teaching. Having done this, and having declared the Buddha's position to be unique, Ambedkar proceeds, in the second section of his article, to compare Buddhism and Hinduism. In so doing, he limits himself to two points, one regarding the position of morality and the meaning of the word Dhamma (or Dharma) and the other regarding the question of equality versus inequality.

With regard to the position of morality Ambedkar exhibits the contrast between the two religions in the boldest and starkest terms. 'Hinduism', he says bluntly, 'is a religion which is not founded on morality.'[9] This is not to say that in Hinduism there is no morality at all but rather that whatever morality Hinduism has is not an integral part of it, but a separate force which is sustained by social necessities and not by injunctions of the Hindu religion. With Buddhism the exact opposite is the case. 'The religion of the Buddha is morality. It is imbedded in religion. Buddhist religion is nothing if not morality. It is true that in Buddhism there is no God. In place of God there is morality. What God is to other religions morality is to Buddhism.'[10] This could hardly have been better or more strongly put, though it is important to understand that Ambedkar is not using the word morality in a narrow, legalistic sense but as representing the whole ethical and spiritual dimension of human existence. The fact that in Buddhism morality takes the place of God means that in Buddhism God is subordinated to morality, not morality to God. It means that actions are to be performed or not performed, not according to whether they are, or are not, commanded by

God, but according to whether they are, or are not, right or wrong or, in Buddhist terms, skilful or unskilful. God's commands are, of course, contained in the infallible scriptures which constitute his 'word'. The fact that in Buddhism morality takes the place of God therefore also means that in Buddhism the infallible scriptures too are subordinated to morality, as well as God, and that one is perfectly free to reject those scriptures if their injunctions conflict with the requirements of morality. Indeed, it is one's duty to reject them. In the case of Hinduism it is the Vedas that are the infallible scriptures, and the Buddha rejected the Vedas because they enjoin the performance of rituals involving animal sacrifice and because animal sacrifice contravenes the principle of non-violence or reverence for life.

Not only did the Vedas enjoin the performance of rituals involving animal sacrifice, but according to the Brahmins the performance of such rituals constituted Dharma (or Dhamma), that is, constituted religion. As Ambedkar observes, 'The Dharma as enunciated by the Brahmins and as propounded in the Purvamimamsa of Jaimini [is] nothing more than the performance of certain Karmas or, to use the terminology of the Roman religion, observances. Dharma to Brahmins meant keeping up observances, i.e. Yajnas, Yagas, and sacrifices to Gods. This was the essence of the Brahmanic Vedic Religion. It had nothing to do with morality.'[11] For the Buddha, of course, the performance of Vedic rituals was far from constituting Dharma. According to him, the essence of Dharma or religion was not Yagas or Yajnas but morality. Thus, 'although the word Dhamma was used both by Brahmanic teachers as well as by the Buddha, the content of both is radically different.'[12] The Buddha in fact gave the word Dhamma what Ambedkar has earlier called 'a most revolutionary meaning', and the latter therefore concludes that 'the Buddha was the first teacher in the world who made morality the essence and foundation of religion.'[13] Be that as it may (for the transition from ethnic to universal religion was everywhere accompanied by a redefinition of key terms), there is no doubt that in Buddhism the word Dhamma (or Dharma) has a totally different meaning from what it has in Hinduism and that unless this is understood the contrast between the two religions will not be fully appreciated.

With regard to the question of equality versus inequality, the second of the two points to which Ambedkar limits his comparison of Buddhism and Hinduism, the contrast between the two religions is exhibited no less boldly and starkly than it was in the case of the first point. Going straight to the heart of the matter, Ambedkar declares that 'the official gospel of Hinduism is inequality',[14] and that the concrete embodiment of this gospel of inequality is the doctrine of Chaturvarna or the doctrine that (Indian) humanity is divided into four divinely ordained hereditary classes in accordance with their innate superiority or inferiority to one another. These four classes are, of course, those of the Brahmin or priest, the Kshatriya or warrior, the Vaishya or trader, and the Shudra or menial, that is, the four classes of which the 2,000 or more hereditary castes of Hindu society are at least theoretically the subdivisions, so that the doctrine of Chaturvarna is in principle the doctrine of the caste system. As against the gospel of inequality and its concrete embodiment the doctrine of Chaturvarna the Buddha stood for equality and was, in fact, the greatest opponent of Chaturvarna. 'He not only preached against it, fought against it, but did everything to uproot it. According to Hinduism neither a Shudra nor a woman could become a teacher of religion nor could they take *Sannyasa* [or initiation into the ascetic life] and reach God. Buddha on the other hand admitted Shudras into the Bhikshu Sangha. He also admitted women to become Bhikshunis. Why did he do this? Few people seem to realize the importance of this step. The answer is that Buddha wanted to take concrete steps to destroy the gospel of inequality.'[15] But though Ambedkar rightly represents the Buddha as standing for equality and opposing the gospel of inequality and taking concrete steps to destroy it, he certainly does not think that the Buddha believed that all men are equal in the sense of believing that they are identical in all respects and, therefore, interchangeable. Ambedkar himself did not believe any such thing. As he had made clear as far back as 1936, in his undelivered address on 'Annihilation of Caste', even though the objections to equality are sound, and even though all men are not equal, one must still accept equality as the governing principle of social life. Standing for equality, therefore, means treating men as equal even though they are in fact not equal. If they are treated as equal even though they are not equal society will get more out of them—which obviously will be to society's advantage. Moreover, since people are unequal in so many ways it is not possible to classify them and since they cannot be classified it is impossible to treat them according to their need or capacity. For this reason the statesman, who is concerned with vast numbers of people, has no alternative but to follow the rough and ready rule of treating everyone alike.[16]

Since Buddhism is free from the evil of not being founded on morality and from the evil of inequality it is hardly surprising that, in modern times, some people should believe that only the acceptance of the Gospel of the Buddha can save the Hindus. Some of them are filled with sorrow, however, because they do not see much prospect of the return of Buddhism to India or its revival there. Ambedkar does not share this pessimism, and in the third section of 'The Buddha and the Future of His Religion' he not only says that he does not share it but explains why. He does not share it for two reasons. In the first place, though there are some Hindus for whom Hinduism is true because all religions are true (a thesis than which, according to Ambedkar, no thesis can be more false) there are other Hindus who have come to realize that there is something wrong with their religion. For one reason or another, however, they are not ready either to denounce Hinduism openly or to abandon it; nor are they ready openly to embrace Buddhism. In some cases they console themselves with the thought that since all religions are wrong there is no point in bothering about religion anyway. Such an attitude on the part of the Hindus, Ambedkar believes, can only have one result. 'Hinduism will lapse and cease to be a force governing life. There will be a void which will have the effect of disintegrating the Hindu society. Hindus will then be forced to take a more positive attitude. When they do, they can turn to nothing except Buddhism.'[20] In the second place, Hinduism gives no mental or moral relief to the millions of people belonging to the so-called Backward Classes or Scheduled Castes, and it is therefore futile for the Hindus to expect these people to go on living under Hinduism. The truth is that Hinduism is sitting on a volcano which, though today it appears to be extinct, will become active once 'these mighty millions become conscious of their degradation and know that it is largely due to the social philosophy of the Hindu religion.'[21] Ambedkar is reminded of the overthrow of Paganism by Christianity in the days of the Roman Empire. 'When the masses realized that Paganism could give them no mental or moral relief they gave it up and adopted Christianity. What happened in Rome is sure to happen in India. The Hindu masses when they are enlightened are sure to turn to Buddhism.'[22]

It is perhaps because he is optimistic rather than pessimistic about the prospect of the return of Buddhism to India, as well as for other reasons, that in the fourth section of his article Ambedkar does not take the other non-Hindu religions and compare them with Buddhism but, instead, puts his conclusions in summary form. This he does by stating the three requirements which a religion must fulfil and the extent to which, in his opinion, the existing religions fulfil them. Before he can state his three requirements, though, Ambedkar has to show that religion is necessary. In doing this he takes for his point of departure the fact that society must have something to hold it together. What holds it together, he maintains, is 'either the sanction of law or the sanction of morality,'[23] for deprived of either of these society is sure to fall to pieces. In all societies, however, law plays a very small part, being intended to keep the anti-social minority under control and prevent it from disrupting the social order. The majority is necessarily left to sustain its social life by means of what Ambedkar calls 'the postulates and sanction of morality'.[24] It is for this reason that religion, in the sense of morality, must remain the governing principle of any society, and it is because it is the governing principle of every society that it is necessary. Having shown this, Ambedkar is in a position to state the three requirements which religion—in the sense in which he has defined it—must fulfil. It must be in accord with science, it must recognize the fundamental tenets of liberty, equality, and fraternity, and it must not sanctify and ennoble poverty.

Ambedkar's character and personal background being what

they were, it is not difficult to see why he should have thought it necessary for religion to fulfil these three requirements, and in his brief comments on them he does in fact provide us with a few clues to his thinking. As one who had spent seven of the most impressionable years of his life in the West, and indeed had received his higher education there, he was well aware how immense was the prestige of science and how great the extent of its influence in the modern world. Having declared that religion must be in accord with science, he therefore goes on to explain that unless religion accords with science 'it is bound to lose its respect and therefore become the subject of ridicule and thereby not merely lose its force as a governing principle of |social| life but might in course of time disintegrate and lapse.'[25] In saying that religion must be in accord with science Ambedkar does not, of course, mean that it is possible to demonstrate the truth of religion scientifically, or that there is nothing in religion which is not susceptible to scientific investigation. (In Buddhism the Dharma is said to be atakkavachara or 'beyond reason' and for Ambedkar science and reason are synonymous.) What he means is that what does not accord with science, in the sense that it can be actually disproved on scientific grounds, cannot be accepted as religion even though it may traditionally be regarded as such.

Recognition of the tenets of liberty, equality, and fraternity is a requirement of religion because the three are fundamental principles of social life and 'unless a religion recognize these three fundamentals of social life religion will be doomed'.[26] These are strong words indeed, but there is no doubt that Ambedkar realized—as many people have come to realize in this century, especially in the West—that unless religion can show that it has a social conscience and that it is actively involved in the struggle for social justice it will not be taken seriously by thinking men and women. Ambedkar's own commitment to the principles of liberty, equality, and fraternity seems to have gone back a long way, even though he at first saw in them only 'the slogan of the French Revolution'. Later in life, when he had immersed himself in the study of Buddhism for some years, he came to see that their roots were in fact religious rather than political and that they could be derived from the teachings of the

Buddha. His most detailed treatment of them is to be found, however, in his undelivered address on 'Annihilation of Caste', to which reference has already been made. Half way through this address, having told 'the tiresome tale of the sad effects that caste has produced' he turns to the constructive side of the problem to consider the ideal society. His own ideal society, he says, would be a society based on liberty, equality, and fraternity. Taking the three in reverse order, he declares he cannot imagine any objection to fraternity, for an ideal society should be mobile, should be full of channels for conveying changes taking place in one part of society to other parts. 'In an ideal society there should be many interests consciously communicated and shared. There should be varied and free points of contact with other modes of association. In other words there must be social endosmosis.'[27] This is fraternity, which Ambedkar believes is only another name for democracy, for democracy is not merely a form of government but is primarily a mode of associated living, of conjoint communicated experience. In fact democracy 'is essentially an attitude of respect and reverence towards [one's] fellow men'.[28] As for liberty, there can surely be no objection to that either. But liberty does not mean only the right to life and limb, or the right to property, tools, and materials as being necessary to the earning of one's living. There must also be the right to make full use of one's powers, and this must include the right to choose one's profession—a right which the caste system denies. In the case of equality there may indeed be objections, and these objections may be sound, but—as we saw in connection with the question of equality versus inequality—Ambedkar believes that for a variety of practical reasons equality has to be accepted as a governing principle of social life.

Poverty is one of the curses of humanity, and in declaring that religion must not sanctify or ennoble poverty Ambedkar gives full recognition to this fact. By poverty he does not mean voluntary poverty of the kind exemplified by the Buddha, Milarepa, and St Francis of Assisi, for he is prepared to recognize that 'renunciation of riches by those who have it may be a blessed state'.[29] In requiring of religion that it must not sanctify and ennoble poverty what Ambedkar has in mind is the bitter, grinding poverty that is imposed on people against their will either by force of circumstances or by the greed and selfishness of their so-called fellow men. Poverty of this degrading and demoralizing kind—such as he had studied at first hand and in which the vast majority of Untouchables still lived—in his opinion can never be a blessed state and to declare it to be a blessed state 'is to pervert religion, to perpetuate vice |and| crime, to consent to make earth a living hell'.[30] Hinduism had certainly perverted religion in this way, for in its view both Shudras and Untouchables had no right to wealth and the Caste Hindus were performing a religious duty, so to speak, in depriving them of the little they were able to acquire. Even today, thirty years after Ambedkar's death, reports appearing in the Indian press testify to the fact that untouchable prosperity is still regarded as an affront by the Caste Hindus and still visited, on occasion, with condign punishment.

Such, then, are the requirements that religion as a code of social morality must fulfil. It must be in accord with science, it must recognize the fundamental tenets of liberty, equality, and fraternity, and it must not sanctify or ennoble poverty. Having stated these requirements, Ambedkar has only to consider the question of which religion fulfils all the tests he has proposed. In so doing, he confines himself to existing religions, for in his opinion 'the days of the Mahatmas are gone and |since| the world cannot have a new religion [it] will have to make its choice from those that exist'.[31] Not surprisingly, he believes that the only religion that the world can have is Buddhism. Some religions may satisfy one of the tests, some may even satisfy two, but so far as he knows, Ambedkar declares, only Buddhism satisfies them all, so that if the new world—which is very different from the old world—is to have a religion—and it needs a religion far more than the old world did—then it can only be the religion of the Buddha. The claim is a big one, and Ambedkar is conscious that 'all this may sound very strange'.[32] However, he attributes the strangeness to the fact that most of those who had written about the Buddha had propagated the mistaken idea that the only thing that he taught was Ahimsa or non-violence. Though it is true that the Buddha did teach Ahimsa—and

Ambedkar does not want to minimize its importance, for it is a great doctrine and the world cannot be saved unless it follows it—he nonetheless wishes to emphasize that the Buddha taught many other things besides Ahimsa. 'He taught as part of his religion, social freedom, economic freedom and political freedom. He taught equality, equality not between man and man only but between man and woman.'[33] In short, 'It would be difficult to find a religious teacher to compare with Buddha whose teachings embrace so many aspects of the social life of a people and whose doctrines are so modern and whose main concern was to give salvation to man in his life on earth and not to promise it to him in heaven after he is dead!'[34] With this enthusiastic tribute the fourth section of 'The Buddha and the Future of His Religion' concludes.

If only Buddhism fulfils all the requirements of religion, and if only Buddhism can therefore be the religion of the new world, then obviously Buddhism must be spread as widely as possible. But how can it be spread? In the fifth and last section of his article Ambedkar addresses himself to this question. Believing as he did that the Buddha wished his religion not to be encumbered with the dead wood of the past and that he had given his followers the liberty to chip and chop as the necessities of the case required, it is not surprising that the future convert to Buddhism should suggest some radical changes. If the ideal of spreading Buddhism is to be realized, then in his opinion three steps are 'quite necessary'.[35] These are: To produce a Buddhist Bible; to make changes in the organization, aims, and objects of the Bhikshu Sangha, and to set up a world Buddhist Mission.

The foremost of these needs is the production of a Bible of Buddhism. As Ambedkar says, Buddhist literature is a vast literature and it is impossible to expect a person who wants to know the essence of Buddhism to 'wade through the sea of literature'.[36] He is also of the opinion that the greatest advantage that the other religions have over Buddhism is that each has a gospel which everyone can carry with him and read wherever he goes, that Buddhism suffers from not having such a 'handy gospel', and that the Indian *Dhammapada* has failed to perform the function which such a gospel is expected to perform. While it may indeed be impossible for even the greatest scholar to have an intimate acquaintance with the entire extent of Buddhist canonical literature in Pali, Sanskrit, Tibetan, and Chinese one must not overlook the fact that the essence of Buddhism—in the sense of the fundamental principles of the Dharma—can be known from a number of works, and even chapters of works, both canonical and non-canonical, such as the *Sutta-nipata*, the *Diamond Sutra*, Shantideva's *Bodhicharyavatara* or 'Entry into the Life of Enlightenment', the *Milarepa Kah Bum* or 'Hundred Thousand Songs of Milarepa', and Hakuin's 'Song of Meditation'. One must also not forget that Buddhism spread throughout the whole of Asia without the help of any 'handy gospel' of the Christian or Islamic type, and that its success may not have been unconnected with the fact that in place of a single gospel it had a variety of gospels (in the literary not the doctrinal sense), some of which appealed to one kind of devotee and some to another. But regardless of whether or not Buddhism suffers from not having a handy gospel—and it cannot be denied that fresh compilations from the Buddha's teaching may not be needed from time to time—such a gospel can never be regarded as authoritative for all Buddhists in the way that the Bible is authoritative for all Christians. The Bible is the Word of God. It is a divinely inspired and hence infallible guide to human belief and conduct which, on account of its supernatural origin, reason is powerless to question. Buddhist canonical literature, on the other hand, is the record of the life and teaching of a 'common man' who, after attaining Enlightenment by his own human efforts, 'preached his gospel as a common man'. As Ambedkar has already shown, since the Buddha did not claim to be either the son or the messenger of God, much less still God himself, he never claimed any supernatural sanction, or divine authority, for his teaching, and since he never claimed any supernatural sanction for his teaching that teaching was not to be regarded as infallible. Not being infallible it did not have to be accepted unquestioningly and could even be revised or, in Ambedkar's language, chipped and chopped as the necessities of the case required. Thus between the Bible or Word of God and Buddhist canonical literature or the record of the Buddha's life and teaching there is an enormous difference, and for this reason it would be inappropriate, and perhaps misleading, to describe a gospel culled from the latter as a Buddhist Bible. The connotations of the term 'Bible' and the connotations of 'Buddhist canonical literature' belong, in fact, to two completely different systems of ideas, or worlds of thought, and strictly speaking it is no more possible for us to have a Buddhist Bible than it is possible for us to have a Buddhist Veda or a Buddhist Qur'an.

Though in the previous section of his article Ambedkar has insisted that religion must be in accord with science or reason, he is far from thinking that religion should therefore be devoid of emotional appeal. Explaining why, in his opinion, the Indian *Dhammapada* fails to perform the function of a handy gospel, he makes the interesting and important point that 'Every great religion has been built on faith', by faith apparently meaning not simply blind belief but the emotional-devotional as distinct from the rational component in human nature or, in more concrete terms, the heart as distinct from the head. Nor is that all. Not only has every great religion been built on faith, but 'faith cannot be assimilated if presented in the form of creeds and abstract dogmas',[37] that is, cannot be assimilated if presented in conceptual terms which, by their very nature, appeal to the reason rather than to the emotions. Hence faith 'needs something on which imagination can fasten, some myth or epic or gospel—what is called in journalism a story'.[38] It is because the (Indian) *Dhammapada* 'is not fastened around a story' and seeks, according to Ambedkar, to build faith on abstract dogma, that it fails to perform the function of a handy gospel. From this it is clear that what Ambedkar means by a handy gospel is, in principle, simply the essence of Buddhism presented in imaginative form or in a form that appeals to the deeper, non-rational element in human nature. It is therefore not surprising that in his opinion the proposed gospel of Buddhism should contain a short life of the Buddha, the 'Chinese' *Dhammapada*, some of the important dialogues of the Buddha, and Buddhist ceremonies for birth, initiation, marriage, and death. Of these the life of the Buddha would appeal to the imagination, while the

'Chinese' *Dhammapada*—which as translated by Beal comprises both stories and moral precepts—would appeal to both imagination and reason. Thus a considerable portion of the proposed gospel of Buddhism is in a form that imagination can grasp and in a form, therefore, that makes possible the 'assimilation' or development of faith.

But if faith 'needs something on which the imagination can fasten', it is no less true that the 'myth or epic or gospel' on which imagination fastens has to find expression in an appropriate and aesthetically satisfying form. Having indicated what the proposed gospel of Buddhism should contain, Ambedkar therefore insists that, in preparing such a gospel, the linguistic side of it must not be neglected. 'It must make the language in which it is produced live. It must become an incantation instead of being read as an ethical exposition. Its style must be lucid, moving and must produce an hypnotic effect.'[39] In laying down these requirements Ambedkar may have had in mind the majestic rhythms of the Authorized Version of the Bible (a moving passage from which heads the dedication to *What Congress and Gandhi have done to the Untouchables*) or the refined imagery and exquisite diction of Ashvaghosha's *Buddhacharita* or poetic 'Life of the Buddha', extracts from which he was to include in *The Buddha and His Dhamma*. He may even have had in mind the noble eloquence of those episodes from the *Ramayana* and the *Mahabharata* which, as a boy, he had heard his intensely religious father reading and reciting every evening. Whatever the case may have been, Ambedkar's insistence that the language of his proposed gospel should be living and incantory shows that, despite his own rather unadorned manner of writing, he was sensitive to the magic of style and fully aware of its importance. It might even be said that for Ambedkar a gospel is not really a gospel unless it is, at the same time, literature in the most exalted sense of the term. The beauty of the casket must correspond to the value of the jewels it contains.

Though the production of a Buddhist Bible—in the sense of a presentation of the essence of Buddhism in imaginative form—is the foremost need it does not follow that it represents the most radical change. The most radical change is represented by the second of the three steps which, in Ambedkar's opinion, are quite necessary if the ideal of spreading Buddhism is to be realized, namely: To make changes in the organization, aims, and objects of the Bhikshu Sangha or Monastic Order. For many 'born Buddhists' in the Buddhist countries of Asia the idea of making even the slightest change in the constitution of the Bhikshu Sangha is unthinkable. Popular belief, both monastic and lay, insists that the Vinaya or Monastic Code was laid down, in all its details, by the Buddha himself, and that it has been preserved complete and unaltered down to the present day. As a scholarly student of Buddhism, Ambedkar knew that this was not really the case and that, even in the Theravada countries of south-east Asia, the Vinaya had been altered from time to time, at least in actual practice. With his customary boldness he has, therefore, no hesitation in declaring that changes in the organization, aims, and objects of the Bhikshu Sangha are needed—the more especially since he also believes that the Buddha gave full liberty to his followers to chip and chop as the necessities of the case required.

Before saying what kind of changes in the Bhikshu Sangha he thinks necessary Ambedkar has something to say about the Buddhist Bhikshu and the Buddha's purpose in creating a separate society of Bhikshus. Proceeding from the known to the unknown, he declares that there is the world of difference between a Hindu Sannyasi and a Buddhist Bhikshu. 'A Hindu Sannyasi has nothing to do with the world. He is dead to the world. A Bhikshu has everything to do with the world.'[40] In saying that a Hindu Sannyasi was dead to the world Ambedkar probably had in mind the fact that on the occasion of his initiation into the ascetic life an orthodox Sannyasi performed his own obsequies, which meant that he was thereafter considered civilly dead and his property passed to his heirs. The Bhikshu performed no such obsequies for himself—though this certainly did not mean that in having 'everything to do with the world' he was involved with it in the same way, or for the same reasons, as the ordinary 'worldly' person. The Bhikshu had everything to do with the world in the sense that he was concerned with people's material and spiritual welfare, and it was possible for him to be concerned with people's material and spiritual welfare because though he was not civilly dead to the world, like the Hindu Sannyasi, he was spiritually dead to it in that he was devoid of any mundane interest or ambition. In other words, the Bhikshu had 'everything to do with the world' *out of compassion*—a compassion that was the fruit of wisdom or insight. But though Ambedkar must have realized this he does not dwell upon the point and, having briefly described the difference between the Hindu Sannyasi and the Buddhist Bhikshu, he moves straight on to the question of the Buddha's purpose in creating a separate society of Bhikshus.

According to Ambedkar, the Buddha established the Bhikshu Sangha for three reasons: To provide a model of the ideal society, to create an intellectual elite, and to create a society whose members were free to render service to the people. Though the untouchable leader was 'on his way to embrace Buddhism' he was, at the same time, acutely conscious that it was 'a religion very difficult to practise' and that if its followers were to live up to the ideals embodied in the principles of Buddhism they would need all the help they could get, both personal and institutional. In particular, they would need a model of the ideal society, that is, a model of a society in which people actually practised Buddhism. That model was the Bhikshu Sangha. 'Buddha knew that it was not possible for a common man to realize the Buddhist ideal. But he also wanted that the common man should know what the ideal was and also wanted that there should be placed before the common man a society of men who were bound to practise his ideals. That is why he created the Bhikshu Sangha and bound it down by the rules of the Vinaya.'[41] In saying that it is impossible for a common man to realize the Buddhist ideal Ambedkar no doubt means that it is *difficult* for him to realize it, or that it is impossible for him to realize it while still adhering to his old attitudes and beliefs. If it were literally impossible for a common man to realize the Buddhist ideal, even to a limited extent, then there would be no point in placing the model of an ideal society before him, for a model is meant not simply to be admired but to be imitated. What this in fact implies is that there are degrees in the realization of the ideal, and that those

members of the Buddhist community who have realized it to a
greater extent provide a model for those who have realized it to
a lesser extent. The difference between those who provide a
model and those for whom they provide it does not, however,
necessarily correspond to the formal difference between the
Bhikshus and those whom Ambedkar designates 'the laymen'.

About the Buddha's two other reasons for establishing the
Bhikshu Sangha Ambedkar has little to say, though that little is
of considerable interest. The function of the Bhikshu Sangha as
an intellectual elite being, apparently, 'to give the laymen true
and impartial guidance'[42] he is of the opinion that it was for this
reason that the Buddha prohibited the (individual) Bhikshu from
owning property (other than his three robes, bowl, etc.).
'Ownership of property is one of the greatest obstacles to free
thinking and application of free thought.'[43] This is, perhaps, an
oversimplification of a complex issue or even a half-truth.
Members of the wealthy, property-owning 'Siamese' sub-
division of the Sinhalese branch of the Bhikshu Sangha have
been known to argue that they have greater freedom of thought
and action than their poorer 'Burmese' brethren because the
latter, being economically dependent on the laity, are subject to
pressure from that quarter and are, in consequence, often unable
to speak their minds even on matters directly concerning the
Dhamma. Thus Ambedkar's pronouncement is not altogether
beyond dispute, even though it may be granted that it is essential
that whatever guidance is given by an intellectual elite such as
the Bhikshu Sangha should be true and impartial and that,
therefore, steps ought to be taken to create the conditions
necessary to ensure its truth and impartiality. With regard to the
Buddha's third reason for establishing a Bhikshu Sangha,
Ambedkar is of the opinion that it was because he wanted to
create 'a society the members of which would be free to do
service to the people' that the Buddha 'did not want the Bhikshu
to marry',[44] presumably on the principle that no man can serve
two masters, or because, in the well known words of Sir Francis
Bacon, he that has wife and children has 'given hostages to
fortune'. But though it was because the Buddha wanted him to be
free to serve the people that he did not want the Bhikshu to

marry, this was not the only reason. 'Not marrying' also meant leading a life of chastity, and chastity was an important part of the spiritual life—so much so, indeed, that in Sanskrit and Pali the word brahmacharya or brahmachariya connotes both chastity and the spiritual life itself. This aspect of 'not marrying' Ambedkar does not, however, pursue.

The Bhikshu Sangha thus having been established to provide a model of the ideal society, to create an intellectual elite, and to create a society whose members were free to render service to the people, there arises an important question, a question Ambedkar is not afraid to ask—and to answer. 'Is the Bhikshu Sangha of today living up to these ideals? The answer is emphatically in the negative. It neither guides the people nor does it serve them.'[45] This is, of course, rather sweeping, but Ambedkar has his reasons. Casting his eye over the Buddhist countries of south-east Asia, in particular, the first thing that strikes him is how many Bhikshus there actually are. In fact, in his opinion there are too many Bhikshus and of these, he says, 'a very large majority are merely Sadhus and Sannyasis spending their time in meditation or idleness. There is in them neither learning nor service. When the idea of service to suffering humanity comes to one's mind everyone thinks of the Ramakrishna Mission. No one thinks of the Bhikshu Sangha. Who should regard service as its pious duty? The Sangha or the Mission? There can be no doubt about the answer. Yet the Sangha is a huge army of idlers.'[46] Thus in Ambedkar's view the Bhikshu Sangha of today is not living up to its ideals because its members have, to all intents and purposes, ceased to be Buddhist Bhikshus and become Hindu Sadhus and Sannyasis—a Sadhu being a kind of free-lance Sannyasi who often is no better than an ordinary beggar. In strictly Buddhist terms, the Bhikshus have given up the altruistic Bodhisattva Ideal and adopted the individualistic Arahant ideal, by which is meant not the Arahant ideal taught by the Buddha (which in principle does not differ from the Bodhisattva Ideal) but its later 'Hinayana' distortion. It is no doubt for this reason that Ambedkar describes the majority of Bhikshus as spending their time in 'meditation or idleness', leaving it unclear whether these are alternative occupations or the same thing. By meditation he means, in this context, not the development of calm and insight (shamatha and vipashyana), which between them constitute the royal road to the attainment of Supreme Enlightenment for the benefit of all sentient beings, but rather the subtly individualistic enjoyment of higher states of consciousness for their own sake regardless of the sufferings of the world.

The Ramakrishna Mission, to which Ambedkar so unfavourably compares today's Bhikshu Sangha, was established in 1897 by the famous Hindu preacher Swami Vivekananda with the aim of spreading the teachings of his master, the Bengali mystic Shri Ramakrishna, and the organization was well known in India for its social, educational, and medical work. Ironically enough, Vivekananda had modelled the Order of Sannyasins of Ramakrishna, the ascetic confraternity that conducted the Mission's activities, partly on the ancient Bhikshu Sangha as known to him from the writings of Western orientalists. Ambedkar may not have been aware of this fact. Aware of it or not, when it came to remodelling the ineffective Bhikshu Sangha of today he looked, despite his appreciation of the Ramakrishna Mission's 'service to suffering humanity', not to the Mission but to the Roman Catholic church. Declaring that what was wanted, in place of the 'huge army of idlers', was fewer Bhikshus and Bhikshus who were highly educated, he observed: 'Bhikshus Sangha must borrow some of the features of the Christian priesthood particularly the Jesuits. Christianity has spread in Asia through service—educational and medical. This is possible because the Christian priest is not merely versed in religious lore but because he is also versed in Arts and Science.'[47] The reference to the Jesuits is interesting. They were the missionaries to Asia *par excellence*, and the fully fledged Jesuit was, in the words of a source with which Ambedkar is known to have been familiar, 'a man well over thirty, who for at least a dozen years had been going through a process of formation under strict control, a large part of the time having been spent in study, three years in purely spiritual discipline, and, ordinarily speaking, another long period in the teaching or moral supervision of youth.'[48] The same source goes on to point out that the Jesuit system of training stood 'in acute contrast to the haste with which the earlier monastic and mendicant Orders often bound their members by solemn and irrevocable vows before they were well out of their teens.'[49] Reading these lines Ambedkar would have been reminded of the speed with which the Bhikshu Sangha ordained its own youthful recruits, even though, in the case of Shramaneras and Bhikshus, the vows taken were technically not irrevocable. He would also have known that unlike the Bhikshu the Jesuit was not obliged to wear a special clerical dress on all occasions, so that it was much easier for him to work with and among people and to be accepted by them as one of themselves.

But though Ambedkar believed that inasmuch as the Bhikshu Sangha of today neither guided nor served it could, in its present condition, 'be of no use for the spread of Buddhism', and though he believed that it 'must borrow some features of the Christian priesthood particularly the Jesuits', he was, at the same time, well aware that things had not always been thus. There had been a period when the Buddhist Bhikshu, too, was versed not merely in religious lore but in the arts and sciences. This was really the ideal of the Bhikshus of olden times. As is well known the Universities of Nalanda and Taxila were run and manned by Bhikshus. Evidently they must have been very learned men and knew that social service was essential to the propagation of the faith.'[50] Here Ambedkar clearly sees the ancient Buddhist Sangha as the precursor of both the Ramakrishna Mission and the Jesuits, and he continues with the moving words: 'The Bhikshus of today must return to the old ideal. The Sangha as composed cannot render this [social] service to the laity and cannot therefore attract people to itself.'[51]

This need for the Bhikshus of today to return to the old ideal is closely connected with the third of the three steps which, in Ambedkar's opinion, are necessary if the ideal of spreading Buddhism is to be realized, namely, the setting up a world Buddhist Mission. 'Without a Mission Buddhism can hardly spread. As education requires to be given, religion requires to be propagated.'[52] Though Ambedkar does not go into the question, it is evident from the whole trend of his thinking that his world Buddhist Mission must be either a reformed or revitalized

Bhikshu Sangha, or, if the Bhikshu Sangha is incapable of reforming itself, an entirely new body that will re-create the ancient Buddhist ideal of Sangha or Spiritual Community in a form appropriate to modern conditions. Ambedkar is, of course, fully aware of the practical difficulties that the immense task of setting up a world Buddhist Mission would involve. 'Propaganda cannot be undertaken without men and money. Who can supply these? Obviously countries where Buddhism is a living religion. It is these countries which must find the men and money at least in its initial stages. Will these? There does not seem to be much enthusiasm in these countries for the spread of Buddhism.'[53] Unfortunately, Ambedkar's impression proved to be justified, and during the thirty years that have passed since his death the Buddhist countries of Asia have found few men and little money for propaganda. Least of all have they found either men or money for propaganda in India. Typical of their attitude was the reply of a Thai Bhikshu who, when asked if he and his friends would come and work in India among the newly converted ex-Untouchable Buddhists, replied, 'Why should we work in India? We are quite comfortable in our own country.'

Yet despite the Buddhist countries seeming lack of enthusiasm for the spread of Buddhism Ambedkar believes that, paradoxically, 'the time is quite propitious for the spread of Buddhism'.[54] The reason for this state of affairs is that nowadays religion is no longer simply part of one's inheritance, and one is free to examine its (supposed) merit and virtues. One is even free to reject religion altogether, as many throughout the world have had the unprecedented courage to do, either as the result of the influence of scientific enquiry or as a result of Marxist teaching. Whatever the causes may be, the fact is that people have developed an enquiring mind in respect of religion and the question of whether religion is at all worth having and, if so, which religion is worth having, are questions which according to Ambedkar are uppermost in the minds of those who dare to think about the subject. He is therefore convinced that so far as the spreading of Buddhism is concerned the time has come. 'What is wanted is will. If the countries which are Buddhist can develop the will to spread Buddhism the task of spreading

Buddhism will not be difficult. They must realize that the duty of a Buddhist is not merely to be a good Buddhist. His duty is to spread Buddhism. They must believe that to spread Buddhism is to serve mankind.'[55]

Shortly after sharing his thoughts on 'The Buddha and the Future of His Religion' with the readers of the *Maha Bodhi* and, through them, with Buddhists of the world, Ambedkar left for Ceylon (Sri Lanka), where he attended the inaugural meeting of the World Fellowship of Buddhists, observed Buddhist ceremonies and rituals, and tried to find out to what extent Buddhism was a living religion in Ceylon. In May 1954, and again in December 1954, he visited Burma. From these two Buddhist countries he returned not with the men and the money that were needed for the propagation of Buddhism in India but only with promises of help and (in the case of Burma) an image of the Buddha, which was duly installed in a newly constructed temple at Dehu Road, near Poona. Nonetheless, the great untouchable leader continued to be on his way to embrace Buddhism, and continued to think about Buddhism until, six years after the appearance of his article, the day dawned when he was no longer on his way but had arrived and when thinking about Buddhism was transformed into the reality of Buddhism itself.

7

The Great Mass Conversion

Ambedkar arrived at his spiritual destination, along with nearly 400,000 of his followers, on 14 October 1956, the place being Nagpur. Neither the time nor the place of the great mass conversion, as it came to be called, had been decided upon without a good deal of deliberation. October marked the end of the rainy season, when the weather would neither be very hot (by Indian standards) nor particularly cold, and when it would be easy for people to travel, while that year 14 October happened to be the day of the great Hindu festival of Dassara. According to Hindu tradition Dassara, also known as Vijaya Dasami or 'Victory Tenth', was the anniversary of Rama's triumphant return to his capital after slaying Ravana, the ten-headed demon king of Lanka. It was a festival of lights, for in honour of the hero's return his loyal subjects had illuminated the city with thousands of oil lamps, and on Dassara night devout Hindus still placed rows of oil lamps before their houses. So far as Ambedkar and his followers were concerned, however, Ashoka Vijaya Dasami (as they termed it) commemorated not Rama's return from Lanka but the emperor Ashoka's return from subduing the people of

Kalinga and his subsequent conversion from belief in conquest by means of war (*yuddhavijaya*) to belief in conquest by means of righteousness (*dharmavijaya*). Thus for Ambedkar and his followers, even more than for the Hindus, the festival of Dassara symbolized the victory of the forces of light over the forces of darkness—symbolized, in fact, the victory of Buddhism over Brahmanism.

The place of the great mass conversion was no less significant than its time. The city of Nagpur, then the capital of the State of Madhya Pradesh, was situated exactly in the centre of (divided) India, and in the very region associated—according to some scholars—with the great Buddhist sage Nagarjuna, sometimes called the second founder of Buddhism. Moreover Nagpur, as its name suggested, was the city of the Nagas, and it was the Nagas who, Ambedkar believed, had worked in the beginning for the propagation of Buddhism. As he explained when he addressed the vast gathering on the day following the conversion, the Nagas were non-Aryans, and between the Aryans and the Nagas there existed fierce enmity. 'Many a battle was fought between the Aryans and the non-Aryans. Aryans wanted to completely annihilate the Nagas. There are many legends to be found in the Puranas in this connection. Aryans had burned Nagas [alive]. The sage Agastya saved one Naga and we are supposed to be the descendants of that Naga.' Nor was that all. '[The Nagas] needed a great man to liberate them and they found that great man in the person of Lord Buddha. Bhagwan Buddha saved them from decay and extinction. It was the Nagas who spread the religion of the Buddha throughout the world. . . This is mainly the reason for selecting Nagpur for this great occasion.'[1]

Thus Nagpur was selected instead of Bombay or Sarnath (which at one stage were also under consideration) not just on geographical and historical grounds but for very much deeper reasons. It was selected because Ambedkar believed that he and his followers had their spiritual roots in Nagpur. *'We are supposed to be the descendents of that Naga.'* In these words, at once both humble and proud, we see Ambedkar identifying himself and his followers with the Nagas, and through them with Buddhism, in much the same way as in *The Untouchables* he had identified the Untouchables with those Broken Men who had refused to give up Buddhism and who had been punished by the Brahmins for their refusal. In both cases he was seeking to establish an emotional connection with Buddhism. He was trying to convince himself, and trying to convince his followers, that in embracing Buddhism they were not adopting an alien creed but were simply reclaiming a spiritual heritage of which they had been unjustly deprived and whose existence they had forgotten for centuries.

From this it is obvious how little foundation there was for the accusation that Ambedkar had chosen Nagpur as the venue of the conversion ceremony because it was the headquarters of the Rashtriya Swayamsevak Sangh, a right wing Hindu organization, and because he wanted to annoy them by doing something spectacular right in front of their eyes. As he himself said, this was not true. He had no desire to irritate or provoke anybody by 'scratching his nose' nor did he have any time for such childish pranks. When selecting Nagpur for the historic ceremony he had not had even the remotest idea of the RSS in his mind, and the city had been selected for a reason very different from the one alleged. Ambedkar had, in fact, chosen Nagpur for basically spiritual reasons and these reasons were no more a matter of party politics than the conversion itself was 'only a political stunt' as his opponents afterwards tried to make out.

There was certainly no thought of politics in the minds of the tens of thousands of men, women, and children who, in response to their 'Baba Saheb's' call, left home in the course of the week prior to the ceremony and made their way to Nagpur by train, by motorbus, and by bullock cart from all over the Marathi-speaking areas of central and western India. Those who were unable to find transport travelled the entire distance on foot, with parents and others carrying children who were too young to walk. By whatsoever means they came, all of them, even the poorest, came clad in the spotless white shirts and saris that had been prescribed for the occasion by their beloved leader. Some families had had to sell trinkets in order to buy their new clothes and meet the expenses of the journey, but they had made the sacrifice gladly, and set out for Nagpur with songs on their lips and the hope of a new life in their hearts. Those who were making the journey on foot formed themselves into companies of a hundred or more and marched seven or eight abreast behind men carrying banners inscribed with such slogans as, 'Baba Saheb gives the call: Embrace Buddhism one and all!' and 'Move the heavens, move the earth! Turn to Buddhism and have a new birth!' Every now and then one of the more brazen-throated members of the group would raise a cry of 'Victory to the Lord Buddha! Victory to Baba Saheb Ambedkar!' to which the deep voices of the men and the shrill voices of the women and children would respond with an exultant 'Victory!' that could be heard several miles away. On their arrival at Nagpur railway station, at the motorbus depots, or at the reception posts that had been set up on the roads into the city, the pilgrims—for such they were—were met by members of the Indian Buddhist Society's volunteer corps and given whatever help they needed. Some stayed with relations in the Mahar ghettoes, of which there were three or four dozen in and around Nagpur, while others were accommodated in school buildings that had been taken over for the purpose. Many simply camped on any patch of waste ground they could find and cooked, ate, and slept either in improvised shelters or in the open air. By the end of the week 400,000 men, women, and children had poured into Nagpur, with the result that the population had nearly doubled and the white-clad Untouchables had virtually taken over the city. The Caste Hindus, who were accustomed to think of the Untouchables as dirty and undisciplined, gazed with astonishment at the spectacle of tens upon tens of thousands of clean, decently dressed, well behaved and well organized people in whom they had difficulty in recognizing their former slaves and serfs.

Ambedkar himself arrived by air from Delhi on 11 October accompanied by his wife and N. C. Rattu, his private secretary, and was accommodated in a hotel in the heart of the city. Two days later, on the eve of Vijaya Dasami, he held a press conference at the hotel and made clear his position on a number of issues. The most important of these, from a Buddhist point of view, was the question of which form of Buddhism he would be adopting when he embraced Buddhism. The Caste Hindu press, quick to seize upon any opportunity of sowing dissension among the Buddhists and creating confusion in the minds of Ambedkar's followers, had professed great concern about this matter, but with a few straightforward words the great leader cut through the net in which they were trying to entangle him. His Buddhism would adhere to the tenets of the faith as taught by the Buddha himself, he told the assembled reporters, without involving his people in differences which had arisen on account of Hinayana and Mahayana. His Buddhism would be sort of neo-Buddhism or Navayana. By this Ambedkar did not mean that his Buddhism would be an entirely different form of Buddhism, as distinct from Hinayana and Mahayana as they were distinct from each other, but rather that it would be a Buddhism stripped of the 'dead wood' referred to in 'The Buddha and the Future of His Religion' and based on principles which, having been taught by the Buddha, were the common foundation of Hinayana and Mahayana and, in fact, the foundation of any form of Buddhism deserving of the name. Thus when he and his followers came to embrace Buddhism the next day they would literally be embracing just Buddhism and would, therefore, be becoming neither Hinayanists nor Mahayanists but simply Buddhists. Far from wanting to establish a separate sect in the name of Buddhism they would be joining the world-wide Buddhist spiritual community—though joining it only to the extent that that community was faithful to the teaching of the Buddha.

At his press conference Ambedkar had no time to make all this clear. Most of the reporters not only represented Caste Hindu-controlled newspapers but were themselves Caste Hindus of one kind or another and they wanted to know—or pretended to want to know—why Ambedkar was embracing Buddhism, as though there was a great mystery surrounding the matter which he was unwilling to allow them to penetrate. Provoked by their insincerity, as well as by the hostile manner in which they raised the question of his motives, Ambedkar angrily demanded, 'Why cannot you put this question to yourself and your forefathers as to why I am getting out of the Hindu fold and embracing Buddhism?'[2] By this he meant that he was renouncing

Hinduism and adopting another religion on account of the inhuman treatment he and his fellow Untouchables had for generations suffered at the hands of the Caste Hindus, as the reporters knew perfectly well was the case, though like the vast majority of Caste Hindus they feigned ignorance of the fact. To have admitted that they knew why Ambedkar was embracing Buddhism would have meant admitting that they knew that the responsibility for his departure from the Hindu fold rested fairly and squarely on their own shoulders and on the shoulders of their forefathers and this they could not bring themselves to do. Shifting their ground, the reporters therefore raised the issue of the reserved seats and other concessions to which, as Scheduled Caste Hindus, Ambedkar's followers were legally entitled. Would it not be a disaster if they lost these as a result of giving up Hinduism and embracing Buddhism? But once again Ambedkar answered their question with one of his own. Did they want his people to remain Untouchables, he asked the reporters, simply in order to go on enjoying such 'benefits' as those of reservation? If the latter were, in fact, so highly desirable were the Brahmins, for example, prepared to be Untouchables in order to enjoy them? What the Untouchables were really doing, he added in a more conciliatory tone, was making an effort to achieve manhood, which meant learning to stand on their own feet without the help of concessions. As for their embracing Buddhism, he had once told Mahatma Gandhi that though he differed from him on the issue of Untouchability when the time came he would choose only the least harmful way for the country. 'And that is the greatest benefit I am conferring on the country by embracing Buddhism,' he continued proudly, 'for Buddhism is part and parcel of the Bharatiya culture. I have taken care that my conversion will not harm the tradition of the culture and history of this land.'[3]

This was no more than the truth, and the reporters were therefore obliged to listen in silence as Ambedkar, warming to his theme, went on predict that within the next ten or fifteen years the wave of mass conversion would spread all over the country, and India would become a Buddhist country. The Brahmins would be the last to follow, and let them be the last! If mass conversion on such a scale seemed impossible, he told his silent but obviously sceptical audience, then let them remember how in the days of the Roman Empire the most despised sections of the population had embraced the Christian faith and how Christianity had eventually taken over the mighty Roman Empire itself. Admittedly his followers were at present ignorant, but through his writings and speeches he would educate them in the principles of Buddhism. Poor and ignorant though they were, they at least preferred honour to bread, as their readiness to embrace Buddhism and lose their concessions showed. Yet though prepared to sacrifice their concessions if necessary, his followers were not indifferent to material things and would make every effort to improve their economic condition.

From economics to politics was only a short step, and soon Ambedkar was having to answer questions about the forthcoming general elections, the second to be held since independence, and about his own political position. He wanted to form a new political party, he declared, and he wanted to form it before the elections took place. The new party would be called the Republican Party, and it would be open to all who accepted its three guiding principles of liberty, equality, and fraternity. He himself would be contesting election to the Lok Sabha from a suitable constituency on the Republican Party ticket and he would be fighting for—among other things—the abolition of the newly created bilingual State of Bombay which combined Gujerat and Maharashtra. With this end in view he extended his wholehearted support to the Samyukta Maharashtra Samiti, which was fighting for a united Maharashtra with the city of Bombay as its capital.

But even when the press conference was over and the largely unsympathetic reporters had left, Ambedkar, tired though he was, had still not finished with politics—or rather, politics had still not finished with him. Some of the younger and more ambitious of his lieutenants, afraid that conversion to Buddhism would spoil their chances of getting into the Lok Sabha, did their utmost to prevail upon their sixty-four-year-old leader to postpone the conversion ceremony until after the elections. For Ambedkar this was absolutely out of the question. There were upwards of half a million Untouchables in Nagpur, all eagerly looking forward to the following day as the greatest day of their lives, and it was unthinkable that he should disappoint them. Moreover, he was a very sick man, and if the conversion ceremony was not held as planned it would perhaps not be held at all. To these and other arguments the lieutenants in question turned a deaf ear and in the end a deeply distressed Ambedkar had no alternative but to assert his authority. He had made up his mind once and for all, he told them as he dismissed them from his presence, and no power on earth was going to stop him embracing Buddhism the following day. They could embrace it or not embrace it with him as they pleased, but if they decided not to embrace it they would have to take the consequences. Overawed, they withdrew their objections and took leave of their great leader with assurances of their unqualified support.

Wednesday 14 October dawned calm and bright, with a sky of unbroken blue. Having awoken early, Ambedkar asked Rattu to arrange for a hot bath and then to go and see if arrangements for the forthcoming ceremony were complete. On his return the faithful secretary reported that all was well and that vast crowds of white-clad people could be seen streaming towards the Diksha Bhumi or Initiation Ground from every part of the city. They had, in fact, been on the move for several hours, though early as they were the sweepers had been up even earlier, sweeping the road at daybreak and making sure that not a speck of dirt would be visible when their great emancipator passed that way. What was more, as an increasingly brilliant sun rose higher in an increasingly blue sky, and as the vast crowds slowly converged on the Diksha Bhumi in a solid mass of white-clad humanity, the shouts of 'Victory to the Lord Buddha!' and 'Victory to Baba Saheb Ambedkar!' became so loud that they could be heard even in the remotest parts of the city.

At exactly 8.30 a.m. Ambedkar, wearing a white silk dhoti and knee-length coat, left by car for the Diksha Bhumi with his wife, who was wearing a white sari, and Rattu. The Diksha Bhumi was a fourteen-acre enclosure situated on an expanse of open ground near the Vaccine Institute at Shraddhanand Peth. At the northern end of the enclosure stood a roofed-in stage hung on three of its sides with white cloth and surmounted by the hemispherical form of a replica of the Sanchi Stupa, so that it looked like a great white marquee open down one of its longer sides. On Ambedkar's arrival at the Diksha Bhumi, which was gaily decorated with bunting and with the five-hued international Buddhist flag, a wave of excitement passed through the vast gathering, and so eager were those nearest the gangway to get a glimpse of their hero, or even to touch his feet, that his progress to the stage was seriously delayed. Having at length reached it, and having been assisted up the steps, he stood facing his people with bowed head and half-closed eyes, one hand grasping a bamboo staff while the other rested on Kattu's shoulder—the very picture of a pilgrim who has well nigh reached the end of his journey. For an instant the crowd was silent, then broke into thunderous applause. It was now 9.15 a.m. Silently acknowledging the ovation, Ambedkar took his seat near the centre of the stage in between his wife and the wrinkled, russet-robed U Chandramani, the oldest and seniormost Bhikshu in India, whom he had invited specially to Nagpur to officiate at the ceremony. To the right of U Chandramani stood a small table, and on the table there was a gleaming brass Buddha-image flanked by two bronze-gilt chinthés. In front of this improvised shrine incense was burning. Seated behind Ambedkar and U Chandramani were Devapriya Valisinha, the Sinhalese General Secretary of the Maha Bodhi Society, in white Indian shirt and lungi, together with Venerable Sangharatana and three other Sinhalese Bhikshus belonging to the Society, all of them resplendent in bright yellow robes. To the rear of the stage, as well as to the right of the Buddha-image and the left of Mrs Ambedkar, sat and stood leading members of the Scheduled Caste Federation and the Indian Buddhist Society—among them some of the young politicians who had wanted Ambedkar to postpone the conversion ceremony until after the general elections.

In accordance with Indian custom, the proceedings opened with a song, and on this occasion the song was, not unnaturally, in praise of Ambedkar. When it was over the entire gathering stood for a minute's silence in memory of Ambedkar's father, who had died more than forty-three years earlier and without whose constant encouragement the gifted young Bhimrao Ramji might never have grown up to be the leader and emancipator of his people—might never have led them to the promised land of Buddhism. Honour having been paid where honour was due, the actual conversion ceremony could now begin. As four hundred thousand pairs of eyes followed their every movement, the white-clad Ambedkar and his wife rose and stood before U Chandramani with their hands joined in the traditional 'lotus bud' and heads slightly bowed. U Chandramani, who was seated crosslegged on his chair, then recited the time-honoured formula of 'Going for Refuge' to the Buddha, the Dharma, and the Sangha. '*Buddham saranam gachchhami*,' the old man intoned in his impeccable Pali, from which more than fifty years of residence in India had removed all trace of a Burmese accent, '*Dhammam saranam gachchhami, Sangham saranam gachchhami*'; and Ambedkar and his wife, their heads turned in the direction of the gleaming brass Buddha image, repeated the formula three times after him. Though the vast gathering was not aware of the fact, it had originally been Ambedkar's intention to take only the first and second refuges, since in his view the present day Bhikshu Sangha was part of the 'dead wood' that would have to be removed if Buddhism was to spread and taking refuge in it was therefore a waste of time. Devapriya Valisinha, who at Ambedkar's suggestion had arrived in Nagpur early, had however pointed out to him that if he and his followers did not take refuge in the Sangha, as well as in the Buddha and the Dharma, they would not be recognized as Buddhists by the rest of the Buddhist world and the great leader had therefore eventually changed his mind. Besides this more practical consideration there was also the point that—as Ambedkar may have known—the Sangha to which one goes for Refuge is not the Bhikshu Sangha or Monastic Order as such but the Arya Sangha or 'Spiritual Community' of all those who, whether in the past, the present, or the future, and whether as monks or nuns or as laymen or laywomen, have attained one or another of the stages of the Transcendental Path. Thus it was that when U Chandramani recited '*Sangham saranam gachchhami*,' Ambedkar and his wife repeated it after him and Valisinha, who was seated only a few yards away, breathed a sigh of relief. After the Refuges came the Precepts, and repeating the formula for these, too, after U Chandramani, the pair undertook to abstain from harming living beings, from taking the not-given, from sexual misconduct, from false speech, and from indulgence in intoxicating drinks and drugs. Twenty-one years after his declaration that though he had been born a Hindu he would not die a Hindu Ambedkar had redeemed his pledge. He was now a Buddhist, and as he and Savita Ambedkar bowed three times before the image of the Buddha and offered white lotus flowers the great assembly gave expression to its feelings on the occasion with full throated cries of 'Victory to the Lord Buddha!' and 'Victory to Baba Saheb Ambedkar!' The time was 9.45 a.m.

But though he had gone for Refuge to the Three Jewels in the traditional manner and was now a Buddhist, Ambedkar had one thing more to do before the ceremony was, for him, complete. As soon as his closest supporters had garlanded him and Valisinha had presented him with a Sarnath style image of the Buddha, he therefore again rose to his feet and repeated a series of twenty-two vows which he had drawn up specially for the occasion. In these vows he pledged himself not to believe in the gods and goddesses of Hinduism or to worship them, not to regard the Buddha as an incarnation of Vishnu, not to perform the traditional Hindu rites for the dead, and not to employ Brahmins to conduct religious ceremonies, as well as—more positively—to believe in and seek to establish the equality of men (which amounted to a repudiation of the caste system), to follow the path shown by the Buddha, and to observe the Buddhist precepts. The twenty-two vows were, perhaps, summed up in the last four, in which Ambedkar declared, 'I renounce Hinduism which is harmful to humanity and the advancement and development of humanity because it is based on inequality and adopt Buddhism as my religion. I firmly believe that the Dhamma of the Buddha is the only true religion. I believe that I am experiencing a [spiritual] rebirth. I solemnly declare and affirm that I shall hereafter lead my life according to the principles and teachings of the Buddha and his Dhamma.'[4]

Once or twice in the course of repeating his vows, especially when abjuring the worship of the Hindu gods and goddesses and pronouncing the fateful words 'I renounce Hinduism' the great leader seemed greatly moved, his voice choking slightly as he spoke. At such moments he was, no doubt, experiencing a variety of conflicting emotions, from joy and thankfulness at his liberation from Hinduism to bitter regret and even resentment at the thought of all the misery and degradation that he and his people had had to endure at the hands of the followers of that religion.

These emotions did not, however, last very long. His conversion to Buddhism having been completed to his own satisfaction, Ambedkar turned to the 400,000 white-clad figures sitting below him in the enclosure, men on the right and women and children on the left, and in a voice that boomed and crackled from the loudspeakers called upon all those who wanted to embrace Buddhism to stand up. In response to his call the whole vast gathering rose as one man, hands joined in the traditional 'lotus bud' in readiness, whereupon Ambedkar repeated the first Three Refuges, then the Five Precepts, and finally the twenty-two vows, and as one man the whole vast assembly repeated them after him in loud and joyous tones. Thus in the space of half an hour 400,000 people became Buddhists. Ambedkar had made Buddhist history. Indeed, he had made it in more ways than one. Quite apart from the unprecedented number of people he had brought with him into the Buddhist fold (and he was to bring many more the following day and the day after), thus making possible the revival of Buddhism in India on a scale that the pessimists had thought impossible, he had made Buddhist history by himself administering the Three Refuges and Five Precepts to his followers and by making the twenty-two vows an integral part of the conversion ceremony.

In making Buddhist history in these two ways Ambedkar was not, of course, simply making Buddhist history but also, at the same time, breaking with tradition—or with what had come to be regarded as tradition. In the Buddhist countries of south-east Asia, at least, it was—and still is—unthinkable for a mere layman to administer the Refuges and Precepts in the presence of

Bhikshus. Such a proceeding would have been considered as showing gross disrespect not only to those Bhikshus who were actually present but to the whole Bhikshu Sangha and would not have been tolerated for an instant. The reason for this was not far to seek. What had originally been no more than a difference between those followers of the Buddha who lived as Bhikshus or monks (or as Bhikshunis or nuns) and those followers of the Buddha who lived as Upasakas or laymen (or as Upasikas or laywomen) had in the course of centuries hardened into an actual division between the two groups, with the result that the Bhikshus had come to be regarded as the real Buddhists (the Bhikshunis had by that time dropped out of the picture) and the laity as simply their humble supporters. It was, therefore, the Bhikshus who took the lead in all religious—and sometimes even in political and social—matters and who officiated at all ceremonies. In particular it was the Bhikshus—generally the seniormost one present—who administered the Refuges and Precepts to the laity whenever the latter wished to 'take' them, that is, when they wished to repeat them after a Bhikshu as an act of piety or as a means of affirming their membership of a particular ethnic group. Ambedkar's action in administering the Refuges and Precepts to his followers himself, instead of allowing U Chandramani to administer them, therefore represented a bold and dramatic departure from existing south-east Asian Buddhist praxis and, indirectly, a return to something more in accordance with the spirit of the Buddha's teaching. Indeed, by demonstrating that an Upasaka no less than a Bhikshu could administer the Refuges and Precepts Ambedkar was reminding both the old Buddhists and the new that the difference between those who lived as Bhikshus and those who lived as Upasakas and Upasikas was only a difference, not a division, since all alike went for Refuge to the Buddha, the Dharma, and the Sangha. Thus he was, in effect, asserting the fundamental unity of the whole Buddhist spiritual community, male and female, monastic and lay.

Ambedkar's other break with tradition, namely, his making of the twenty-two vows an integral part of the conversion ceremony, had much the same kind of significance. That too was, in effect, an assertion of the fundamental unity of the whole Buddhist spiritual community. One of the main reasons for the eventual disappearance of Buddhism from India was the fact that although there was an initiation ceremony for monks, whereby they were formally received into the Monastic Order, there was no really-corresponding ceremony for lay people, with the result that many of the latter were unable to identify themselves with the Buddhist spiritual community and the Buddhist spiritual tradition in the way the monks did. The result of this state of affairs was twofold. Not only was the division—as distinct from the difference—between the monks and the lay people exacerbated but the loyalties of the lay people became increasingly divided between Buddhism on the one hand and the various cults of a resurgent Brahmanism on the other. A high proportion of the monks had, moreover, tended to congregate in large monasteries which were economically dependent not—as the monks had been before—on the good will of the local lay Buddhist population but on royal patronage. When these monasteries were destroyed by the Muslim invaders, therefore, and their occupants either killed or dispersed, an already half-Hinduized Buddhist laity fell increasingly under the influence of the Brahmins until, having lost their separate religious identity, they were eventually absorbed into the Hindu community (in the case of the Buddhist Broken Men, as Untouchables) and little or nothing remained to show that there had ever been such a thing as Buddhism in India. Knowing all this as he did, Ambedkar was determined to make sure that history did not repeat itself. Having converted his followers to Buddhism he was determined to make sure that they would remain Buddhists and that they would not, when he was no longer there to guide them, revert to their old ways and be reabsorbed into Hinduism.

Obviously, the only way in which he could do this was to make sure that they actually practised Buddhism (and gave up practising Hinduism). But they could hardly be expected to practise Buddhism unless they felt that they were real Buddhists, not merely supporters of the real Buddhists, and they could hardly be expected to feel that they were real Buddhists unless they felt that they were full members of the Buddhist spiritual community. This meant that they had to be formally received into the Buddhist spiritual community, just as a monk was formally received into the Monastic Order, and that they had to undertake to live as lay followers of the Buddha with the same seriousness as a monk undertook to live as a monk follower. In other words, it meant that in addition to taking the Three Refuges and the Five Precepts they also had to take the twenty-two vows, wherein the implication of taking the Three Refuges and the Five Precepts—that is, the implications of being a Buddhist and a member of the Buddhist spiritual community—were spelled out in some detail. It was this taking of the Three Refuges and the Five Precepts *and* the twenty-two vows that constituted conversion to Buddhism in the full sense, or what Ambedkar termed Dharma Diksha—Initiation into the Dharma.

Thus by his making of the twenty-two vows an integral part of the conversion ceremony Ambedkar did three things. He made it clear that embracing Buddhism meant repudiating Hinduism, he made it clear that a lay Buddhist was a full member of the Buddhist spiritual community (thereby asserting the fundamental unity of that community), and he made it clear that the lay Buddhist, no less than the monk, was expected actually to practise Buddhism. By the time the historic ceremony came to an end at 10.50 a.m. a tired but triumphant Ambedkar was therefore able to leave the Diksha Bhumi knowing that there were now 400,000 more Buddhists in the world than when he arrived there, and that he had placed the revival of Buddhism in modern India on a firm foundation.

What Ambedkar and his followers were doing in Nagpur did not pass altogether unnoticed by the rest of the Buddhist world. Messages of congratulation were received from U Ba Swe, the Prime Minister of Burma, and from U Nu, the former Prime Minister, as well as from a handful of prominent Indian, Sinhalese, and British Buddhists. No such message was received from any of the leading figures of either religious or secular India—not even from Ambedkar's former colleagues in the Cabinet, despite the fact that the Government of India was currently sponsoring the celebration of the 2500th Buddha Jayanti. Eulogizing the Buddha and his teaching from public platforms, and extolling the glories of India's ancient Buddhist heritage, was one thing. Declaring oneself a follower of the Buddha, and actually practising his teaching, was, it seemed, quite another.

The following day, Thursday 15 October, Ambedkar held a second conversion ceremony at the Diksha Bhumi and administered the Three Refuges, the Five Precepts, and the twenty-two vows, to more than a 100,000 people who had arrived too late for the main ceremony, thus bringing the total number of converts to a round half million. The movement of mass conversion to Buddhism that he had so courageously inaugurated was beginning to gain momentum. He was also presented with an address of welcome by the Nagpur Municipal Corporation at the town-hall. On both these occasions Ambedkar spoke at some length, though on rather different topics. Replying to the address of welcome, which gave expression to the Corporation's pleasure at receiving a 'social reformer, philosopher, and erudite constitutionalist like Baba Saheb', he denounced the ruling Congress Party in general, and its leader Pandit Nehru, the Prime Minister, in particular, in the most scathing terms, declaring that the Congress has made a mess of politics and that if it remained in power for long the country would be in flames. At the conversion ceremony he explained to the gathering why he had selected Nagpur as the place of the Dharma Diksha, replied in some detail to the critics who had accused him of misleading his downtrodden, poverty-stricken followers by choosing the path of conversion, declared that self-respect was more important than material gains, warned people that they would have to make sacrifices for Buddhism, recalled his Yeola declaration of 1935, and spoke of the 'enormous satisfaction' and 'unimaginable pleasure' that his conversion had given him. He felt, he said, as though he had been liberated from hell, and he wanted all those who were initiated into Buddhism to have the same experience. 'But I do not want blind followers,' he added sharply. 'I do not like sheep mentality. Those who wish to go for Refuge to the Buddha should do so only after counting the cost, for |Buddhism| is a religion very difficult to practise.'[6]

Among the other subjects on which Ambedkar, out of the

fullness of his heart, spoke on that occasion, was the subject of enthusiasm or inspiration. Without enthusiasm, he told the gathering, life became a mere drudgery, a mere burden to be borne. Without enthusiasm, nothing could be achieved, and the reason for the lack of enthusiasm was the loss of all hope of getting an opportunity to elevate oneself. It was the hopelessness that led to lack of enthusiasm, in which the mind became diseased. In the words of the Maharashtrian poet-saint, 'If a man lacks enthusiasm, either his mind or his body is in a diseased condition.'[7] One who saw no hope of ever escaping from his present misery lacked enthusiasm and was always cheerless. Enthusiasm was created when one breathed an atmosphere in which one was sure of getting the legitimate reward for one's labours. Only then did one feel enriched by enthusiasm and inspiration. Hinduism, which was founded on the twin ideologies of inequality and injustice, unfortunately left no room for the development of enthusiasm. So long as the Untouchables continued to slave under the yoke of Hinduism, which was a diabolical creed, they could have no hope, no inspiration, no enthusiasm for a better life. They might produce a few hundred poor clerks who would do nothing except fill their own bellies but that would be all. The untouchable masses would not gain anything. Consequently the Scheduled Castes could never feel enthusiasm about Hinduism or derive inspiration from it, for 'a man derives inspiration |only| if his mind is free to develop.'[8]

In these few words Ambedkar gave expression to the real significance of the great mass conversion for his followers. By embracing Buddhism they had become free to develop, and since they had become free to develop—socially, economically, culturally, and spiritually—they were able to derive inspiration and to generate enthusiasm. As Buddhists, the ultimate source of their inspiration was, of course, the Three Jewels, but for the vast majority of them its immediate source was the great leader under whose guidance they had gone for Refuge to those Three Jewels. During the six weeks of life that still remained to him they continued to derive inspiration mainly from his actual physical presence among them. After his death they derived inspiration from the memory of his noble example, from the record of his words, and from his published writings. Above all, perhaps, they derived inspiration from the book on which he had worked for a number of years and was in the press at the time of his death: the famous and controversial *The Buddha and His Dhamma*.

8

'The Buddha and His Dhamma'

The work which has been described as Ambedkar's magnum opus was written during the years 1951—1956 and published by the People's Education Society in November 1957, almost a year after the great leader's death. In the preface he wrote for it in March 1956, but which did not appear in print until September 1980, Ambedkar traced the origin of the work to his article on 'The Buddha and the Future of His Religion'. In that article, he recalls, he had argued that the Buddha's religion was the only religion which a society awakened by science could accept and without which it would perish. He had also pointed out that in the modern world Buddhism was the only religion which it must have, if it was to save itself. But Buddhism made only a slow advance, and this was 'due to the fact that its literature is so vast that no one can read it [all] and it has no such thing as a Bible as the Christians have. On the publication of ['The Buddha and the Future of His Religion'] I received so many calls, written and oral, to write such a book. It is in response to these calls, that I have undertaken the task.'[1] The writing of *The Buddha and His Dhamma* was thus an attempt on Ambedkar's part to produce the Buddhist Bible which he had, in his 1951 article, pronounced 'quite necessary' if the ideal of spreading Buddhism was to be realized. Despite his use of the inappropriate term 'Bible', however, Ambedkar was far from regarding *The Buddha and His Dhamma* as possessing any special authority. As he wrote of the work in the (recently published) preface, 'How good it is I must leave it to readers to judge. As for myself, I claim no originality. I am only a compiler. All I hope is that the reader will like the presentation. I have made it simple and clear.'[2]

Ambedkar was not, of course, the first person to be impressed by the vast extent of Buddhist literature, nor even the first to compile a volume of selections for the benefit of the common reader. As early as the ninth century CE the poet-sage Shantideva had compiled—mainly from earlier Mahayana sutras—his *Shiksha-samuchchaya* or 'Compendium of Instruction', and in modern times American and British scholars, in particular, have produced a number of such works. By far the most popular of these was Paul Carus's *The Gospel of Buddha*, published in 1894, which apart from Sir Edwin Arnold's *The Light of Asia* (1879) did more to promote the wider dissemination of Buddhism than any other book. Two years after Carus's best-seller came Henry Clarke Warren's *Buddhism in Translations*, a scholarly work which had a much more limited circulation. After an interval of several decades these pioneering efforts were followed by such well-known anthologies as F. L. Woodward's *Some Sayings of the Buddha* (1925), Dwight Goddard's *A Buddhist Bible* (1932), E. J. Thomas's *Early Buddhist Scriptures* (1935), J. G. Jennings' *The Vedantic Buddhism of the Buddha* (1947), E. Conze's *Buddhist Texts Through the Ages* (1954), and E. A. Burtt's *The Teachings of the Compassionate Buddha* (1955). These works, with most of which Ambedkar was familiar, fall into two groups. There are those anthologies which have been compiled from the Buddhist literature of one particular language and even of one particular school of Buddhism and those which have been compiled from the Buddhist literature of more than one language and of more than one school. A good example of the first kind is Woodward's *Some Sayings of the Buddha*, which consists entirely of translations from the Pali scriptures of the Theravada school, while a good example of the second is Conze's *Buddhist Texts*

Through the Ages, which contains translations from the Pali, Sanskrit, Chinese, Tibetan, Japanese, and Apabhramsa scriptures of the Hinayana, Mahayana, and Vajrayana traditions. Each of these two groups of anthologies falls in its turn into two sub-groups, one consisting of anthologies containing only doctrinal material, the other of anthologies in which material illustrative of the Buddha's actual teaching is interwoven with material illustrative of the story of his life. Probably the best example of an anthology belonging to the first of these two sub-groups is Goddard's *Buddhist Bible*, which consists mainly of (sometimes shortened) versions of a limited number of major Pali, Sanskrit, Chinese, and Tibetan doctrinal and spiritual texts. In terms of popularity, at least, no doubt the best example of an anthology belonging to the second sub-group is Carus's *The Gospel of Buddha*, which, as its title suggests, attempts to do for the founder of Buddhism what the fourth Evangelist, in particular, did for the founder of Christianity.

It is not difficult to see to which group of anthologies, and which sub-group within that group, *The Buddha and His Dhamma* belongs. In the first place, it has been compiled from Buddhist canonical and non-canonical literature, in Pali, Sanskrit, and Chinese, and from texts belonging to the Theravada, Sarvastivada, and Mahayana schools of Buddhism. In the second, it interweaves material illustrative of the Buddha's actual teaching with material illustrative of the story of his life, both of these being further interwoven with what Carus, in the case of *The Gospel of Buddha*, terms 'Explanatory Additions', the Explanatory Additions to *The Buddha and His Dhamma* being of course by Ambedkar himself. Between the work of the American scholar-scientist and the work of the Indian scholar-statesman there is, in fact, a closer resemblance than there is between *The Buddha and His Dhamma* and any of the other anthologies which have been mentioned. Both *The Gospel of Buddha* and *The Buddha and His Dhamma* are divided into eight books (as Ambedkar styles them), each book being subdivided into chapters and verses. More remarkable still, in the case of both works the verses are all numbered, the numbering being separate for each chapter.

But though there are resemblances between *The Buddha and*

His Dhamma and *The Gospel of Buddha* there are also differences. On the whole, the material contained in *The Buddha and His Dhamma* is more systematically organized, and Ambedkar's Explanatory Additions are not only much more numerous than Carus's but more substantial in character. The biggest difference between the two anthologies, however, consists in the fact that they were intended for two very different audiences. Whereas Carus compiled *The Gospel of Buddha* mainly, though not exclusively, for the benefit of relatively affluent and well-educated Americans and Europeans Ambedkar compiled *The Buddha and His Dhamma* mainly, though not exclusively, for the benefit of desperately poor ex-untouchable Indian Buddhists, many of whom were illiterate and would need to have his words orally explained to them in their own vernacular. Moreover, though in his Preface Carus speaks of Christianity in appreciative rather than in critical terms *The Gospel of Buddha* was in fact meant for those who were disillusioned with Christianity, or who did not consider themselves Christians in the orthodox sense. *The Buddha and His Dhamma,* on the other hand, was meant for those who were disillusioned with Hinduism, or who were even in active revolt against it, and the terms in which Ambedkar speaks of Hinduism are definitely critical rather than appreciative. What is perhaps more important still, whereas Carus presents data of the Buddha's life in the light of what he terms its religio-philosophical importance Ambedkar presents them in the light of what may be termed its socio-political importance. Ambedkar's approach to Buddhism thus is social and ethical rather than philosophical and mystical, as even a short account of *The Buddha and His Dhamma* will be sufficient to reveal. Before embarking on such an account, however, we shall have to try and clear up some of the doubts by which the work became surrounded at the time of its original appearance, nearly a year after Ambedkar's death, and which for some of his followers surround it still.

These doubts find expression in two closely related questions: Was *The Buddha and His Dhamma* published in exactly the same form that Ambedkar himself left it at the time of his death? And, had Ambedkar really been able to complete the work in accordance with his original intentions? With regard to the first question, it would appear that the published version of *The Buddha and His Dhamma* differs from Ambedkar's own version in at least one respect, that is, in not including the Preface which he wrote for it on 15 March 1956. This Preface, as we have already seen, did not appear in print until 1980, when Bhagwan Das, a well known Punjabi Buddhist litterateur, included it in his *Rare Prefaces Written by Dr Ambedkar*. But though the Preface itself did not appear in the published version of *The Buddha and His Dhamma* all the points which Ambedkar makes in it concerning his early religious impressions, the origin of the book, and the circumstances under which it had been compiled, were faithfully incorporated in the publishers' Foreword. All the points, that is, except one. This point related to Ambedkar's illness and to the help he had received from his wife and Dr Malvankar. It would therefore appear that the reason why the Preface which Ambedkar had written for *The Buddha and His Dhamma* on 15 March 1956 did not appear in the published version of that work was that it contained a reference to Mrs Ambedkar, for after the great leader's death his widow had become *persona non grata* to many of his followers and the publishers must have decided to omit the Preface out of consideration for their feelings.

With regard to the question of whether Ambedkar had really been able to complete *The Buddha and His Dhamma* in accordance with his original intentions, it is necessary to go back to the speech which he delivered at Dehu Road on 25 December 1955. In that speech he told his audience that he was writing a book explaining the tenets of Buddhism in simple language for the benefit of the common man, that it might take him a year to complete the work, but that when it was finished he would embrace Buddhism. Yet by February 1956 the last chapters of *The Buddha and His Dhamma* had been written and on 15 March he was able to compose his Preface. How was this possible? How had Ambedkar, then a very sick man, been able to complete in less than two months a task that he had thought might take him twelve? One can only assume that, realizing he did not have much longer to live, he had decided that instead of trying to complete *The Buddha and His Dhamma* in accordance with his

149

original intentions he would bring it out just as it was and embrace Buddhism immediately afterwards. He was, in fact, extremely anxious that his book should be published without delay. On 5 May 1956 he wrote to S. S. Rege, the librarian of Siddharth College, Bombay: 'There is one urgent matter which I want you to attend to and that is the publication of my book *The Buddha and His Dhamma*. . . I am in a great hurry and I want the book to be published by September the latest.'[3] The wingèd chariot was hurrying near, and Ambedkar could hear it. Less than three weeks later, on 24 May, he announced that he would embrace Buddhism in October 1956—in other words, a month after the expected publication of his book.

What *The Buddha and His Dhamma* would have been like if Ambedkar had been able to complete it in accordance with his original intentions we can only speculate. There is little doubt, however, that its contents would have corresponded more closely to those of his proposed 'gospel of Buddhism', as described in 'The Buddha and the Future of His Religion', and that in addition to 'a short life of Buddha' and 'some of the important dialogues' it would have contained the 'Chinese' *Dhammapada* and 'Buddhist Ceremonies for birth, initiation, marriage, and death'. There is also little doubt that, in accordance with his own dictum that 'in preparing such a gospel the linguistic side of it must not be neglected',[4] Ambedkar would have given more attention to the literary style of the work. In the form in which we have it, *The Buddha and His Dhamma* is, stylistically speaking, quite rough in texture. This is particularly true of Book III and of Book IV, Parts I and II. Indeed, it is at times difficult to resist the impression that one is reading notes that Ambedkar did not have time to work up properly or which he did not intend for publication—an impression that is reinforced by the fact that he was revising the proofs of the book right up to the time of his death. It is also likely that besides incorporating more material in *The Buddha and His Dhamma* and improving its style Ambedkar would have included a Table of Reference showing the sources he had utilized in compiling the work (as Carus had done in the case of *The Gospel of Buddha*), thus making his book more useful to the serious student.

But speculations of this sort need not be carried too far. Even though Ambedkar was unable to complete *The Buddha and His Dhamma* in accordance with his original intentions it is, nevertheless, a monument to his untiring industry, his exemplary devotion to the Buddha and his teaching, and his heartfelt desire to understand that teaching and relate it to the needs of his people—and it is these things that really matter. *The Buddha and His Dhamma* can, in fact, be compared to a well planned, solidly built, and beautifully decorated palace, some apartments of which the architect was obliged to leave unfinished. Though they are unfinished, so splendid is the palace as a whole, and so perfectly inhabitable, that as one enters the lofty portals and starts looking round one is struck less by any incompleteness in the execution of the work as by the genius of the architect and the grandeur of his overall design.

As we have already seen, *The Buddha and His Dhamma* is divided into eight books, the last four of which are only half the length of the first four. Six of the books are further divided into parts (that is, chapters), sub-sections, and verses, the remaining two books being divided into parts, sections, sub-sections, and verses. Altogether there are 40 parts, 14 sections, 248 sub-sections, and 5013 verses, which between them cover 430 pages. At a rough estimate, three-quarters of the work consists of extracts from—or adaptations of—Buddhist literature both canonical and non-canonical, while the remaining quarter consists of Ambedkar's own Explanatory Additions. In the vast majority of cases, the extracts from the canonical literature are taken from the Sutta- and Vinaya-Pitakas of the Theravada Pali Tipitaka or 'Three Collections' (Ambedkar apparently regarded the Abhidhamma-Pitaka as a later addition), only a few of them being taken from the Mahayana sutras. As for the extracts from the non-canonical literature, most of these are taken from Ashvaghosha's celebrated epic poem the *Buddhacharita* or 'Life of the Buddha', though the Pali commentaries, the *Milinda-panha* or 'Questions of [King] Milinda', and even a Chinese translation of a prayer to Amitabha, the Buddha of Infinite Light, are also laid under contribution.

Book I of *The Buddha and His Dhamma*, entitled 'Siddarth

Gautam—How a Bodhisatta became the Buddha', is mainly, though not exclusively, biographical in character. In the first five parts Ambedkar tells the story of the Buddha's life from his birth to his leaving home and from his leaving home to his attainment of Enlightenment, while in the last three parts he compares the Buddha with his predecessors and contemporaries and explains which of their ideas he rejected, which he modified, and which he accepted in formulating his own teaching. But though Ambedkar tells the story of the Buddha's life from his birth to his leaving home, and from his leaving home to his attainment of Enlightenment, he does not tell it quite in the traditional way. Indeed, he tells it in a very untraditional way. The main reason for this is that he finds it impossible to accept the traditional answer to the question of why the Buddha (or rather the Bodhisattva, as he then was) left home, namely, that he left it as a result of seeing, for the first time, an old man, a sick man, a corpse, and a wandering ascetic. Taking a hint from an apparently autobiographical passage in the *Sutta-nipata*, an ancient text belonging to the fifth division of the Sutta-Pitaka, and combining this with an antedated version of the conflict between the Shakyas, to whom the Buddha was related through his father, and the Koliyas, to whom he was related through his mother, he therefore represents the Buddha-to-be as leaving home as a result of his opposition to the Shakya clan's decision to go to war with the Koliya clan. As told by Ambedkar, the story of this 'crisis in the life of Siddharth', as he calls it, is both consistent and psychologically convincing, as well as of great human interest, especially as his own Explanatory Additions are interwoven with some of the most affecting episodes from Ashvaghosha's *Buddhacharita*. Yet despite its essential truth (for was not the Bodhisattva's preoccupation with the problem of human suffering a preoccupation, at the same time, with the problem of human conflict?) Ambedkar's re-telling of the story of the Buddha's early life is an imaginative reconstruction rather than the product of strictly scientific research. Though accepted by many of his followers it has not, therefore, been taken seriously by Buddhist scholars.

The Buddha's attainment of Enlightenment having been

followed by his decision to preach, in Book II of *The Buddha and His Dhamma* Ambedkar describes the preaching of the First Sermon and the conversion of the five Parivrajakas or wandering ascetics, as well as the conversion of 'the High and the Holy', of the Buddha's own relations, of 'the Low and the Lowly', of women, and of 'the Fallen and the Criminals'. This book is therefore entitled 'Campaign of Conversion'. Before describing the Buddha's 'First Sermon' and the conversion of the five Parivrajakas, however, Ambedkar devotes a short section to the subject of the two types of conversion. In the Buddha's scheme of things, he says, conversion has two meanings. There is conversion to the Order of Bhikkhus and there is a householder's conversion as an Upasaka or lay follower, though 'except on four points there is no difference in the way of life of the Bhikkhu and the Upasaka'.[5] One of these points is that 'to become an Upasaka there is no ceremony'[6]—a deficiency which Ambedkar sought to remedy by drawing up his list of twenty-two vows and administering these to his followers at the time of the great mass conversion. By emphasizing that there are two kinds of conversion and that, therefore, conversion does not (necessarily) mean becoming a monk, as well as by emphasizing that except on four points there is no difference in the way of life of the Bhikkhu and the way of life of the Upasaka, Ambedkar in effect asserts the fundamental unity of the whole Buddhist spiritual community, just as he did by administering the Three Refuges and Five Precepts to his followers himself and making the twenty-two vows an integral part of the conversion ceremony.

According to tradition the Buddha's First Sermon, delivered to the five Parivrajakas in the Deer Park at Sarnath, near Benares, consisted in a brief statement of the Middle Way, the Four Noble Truths, and the Noble Eightfold Path. Ambedkar regards this as quite inadequate. Indeed, besides being doubtful whether the Four Noble Truths formed part of the original teaching of the Buddha he is of the opinion that they are 'a great stumbling block in the way of non-Buddhists accepting the gospel of Buddhism'.[7] In describing the events leading up to the conversion of the five Parivrajakas he therefore represents the Buddha as speaking of the Dharma he had discovered not just in terms of the Middle

Way and in terms of what is, in effect, a 'revised version' of the Four Noble Truths, but also in terms of the Path of Purity, the Path of Righteousness, and the Path of Virtue, which he seems to regard as three successive stages of spiritual development. The Path of Purity consists in recognizing the Five Precepts as principles of life, the Path of Righteousness in following the Noble Eightfold Path, and the Path of Virtue in observing the ten Paramitas or 'States of Perfection' (as he calls them), these last being enumerated according to the Theravada tradition. (In Book I they are enumerated according to the Mahayana tradition, and the Buddha-to-be is represented as practising them seriatim for ten successive lifetimes, whereas the traditional teaching is that he practises them simultaneously over a period of three successive kalpas or aeons.) The preaching of the (revised and enlarged) First Sermon having led the five Parivrajakas to realize that 'this was really a new Dhamma,'[8] the Buddha's campaign of conversion proceeds apace. Among 'the High and the Holy' to be converted are Yashas, the nobleman's son, the three fire-worshipping Kassapa brothers, the young Brahmin seekers Sariputta and Moggallana, subsequently to become the Buddha's chief disciples, King Bimbisara of Magadha, the royal treasurer Anathapindika, and the royal doctor Jivaka, while 'the Low and the Lowly' are represented by Upali the barber, Sunita the sweeper, Sopaka and Suppiya, the Untouchables, Sumangala the peasant, Dhaniya the potter, Kappatakura the grass-seller, and Suppabuddha the leper, all of whom are received into the Order. The Buddha also converts women like his aunt and foster-mother Mahaprajapati Gautami and his former wife Yashodhara, as well as the low-caste girl Prakriti, vagabonds like the unnamed man of Rajagriha, and robbers like the ferocious Angulimala. Not that the Buddha had converted only those whose stories Ambedkar actually relates. As the latter is careful to explain: 'The instances are chosen only to show that he did not observe any distinction as to caste or sex in admitting persons to his Sangh or preaching his Dhamma.'[9] That the Buddha did not observe distinctions of this kind was, of course, one of the principal reasons why Ambedkar and his followers decided to embrace Buddhism and it is therefore natural that he should want to draw particular attention to this feature of the Buddha's teaching.

Book III, entitled 'What the Buddha Taught', and Parts I and II of Book IV, entitled 'Religion and Dhamma', are mainly philosophical in character. Parts III and IV of Book IV, on the other hand, are mainly ethical and psychological. Conscious that there is an astonishing divergence of views regarding Buddhism, Ambedkar is concerned to establish the real nature of the Buddha's teaching. This he does with the help of a classification which the Buddha himself (he believes) had adopted, namely, the classification of Dhamma into the three categories of Dhamma, Not-Dhamma (Adhamma), 'though it [goes] by the name of Dhamma',[10] and Saddhamma which is another name for the philosophy of Dhamma. Dhamma consists in maintaining purity of life (including purity of body, speech, and mind), in reaching perfection in this life (here Ambedkar includes a dialogue between Subhuti and the Buddha taken from the *Panchavimshatisahasrika* or Perfection of Wisdom 'in 25,000 lines'), in living in Nirvana or living free from greed, hatred, and delusion, in giving up craving, in believing that all compound things are impermanent, and in believing that the law of Karma is the instrument of the moral order. Not-Dhamma consists in belief in the supernatural as the cause of events, in the belief that the world was created by God, in the belief that Dhamma is based on union with Brahma, in the belief that sacrifices— including animal sacrifices—are a part of religion, in the belief that speculations regarding the origin of the self and the universe are a part of religion, in the belief that the reading of books is Dhamma, and in belief in the infallibility of sacred books like the Vedas. Finally, the functions of Saddhamma are in the first place to cleanse the mind of its impurities and in the second to make the world a kingdom of righteousness. In order to be Saddhamma, however, Dhamma must promote Prajna or insight, and this it does by making learning open to all, by teaching that mere learning is not enough, as it may lead to pedantry, and by teaching that what is needed is Prajna or right thinking. Moreover, Dhamma is Saddhamma only when it teaches that Prajna must be accompanied by Sila or right action, as well as by Karuna or compassion for the poor and helpless and by Maitri or love for all living beings. From this it follows that, in order to be Saddhamma, Dhamma must break down the barriers between man and man, must teach that worth and not birth is the measure of man, and must promote equality between man and man. Thus Ambedkar establishes the real nature of the Buddha's teaching by, in effect, replacing the traditional triad of Sila, Samadhi, and Prajna by his own triad of Sila, Prajna, and Karuna-Maitri. This enables him to bring out the social implications of the Buddha's teaching more fully and clearly than they had been brought out before and to answer in the affirmative the question, 'Did the Buddha have [a] Social Message?'

Since much of the divergence of views regarding Buddhism is semantic in origin, Ambedkar also explores the nature of the difference between religion and Dhamma, and between their respective purposes, as well as the way in which similarities in terminology with regard to such questions as rebirth, Karma, and Ahimsa or non-killing, may conceal a fundamental difference of outlook. Perhaps the most valuable and important part of his exploration is that in which, having dealt with the relation between Dhamma and religion, he asserts that mere Morality is not enough, but that it must be 'sacred and universal'.[11] Here we encounter some of Ambedkar's deepest thinking. Morality, he asserts, has no place in religion, for religion is concerned with the relation between man and God, morality with the relation between man and man. Though every religion preaches morality, morality comes into religion only in order to help maintain peace and order, and is not the root of religion. '[Morality] is a wagon attached to [religion]. It is attached and detached as the occasion requires.' (If 'God' tells you to do something, morality can be disregarded.) 'The action of morality in the functioning of religion is therefore casual and occasional. Morality in religion is therefore not effective.'[12] So far as Dhamma is concerned the exact opposite is the case. We cannot even say what place morality has in Dhamma, for 'Morality is Dhamma and Dhamma is Morality'.[13] Morality is the essence of Dhamma; without it there is no Dhamma, and 'Morality in Dhamma arises from the direct necessity for man to love man.' Such morality does not require divine sanction. 'It is not to please God that man has to be moral. It is for his own good that man has to love man.'[14] This morality which is Dhamma is not, however, the anti-social morality that serves to protect the interests of a particular group. On the contrary, it is that sacred and universal morality which protects the weak from the strong, which provides common models, standards, and rules, and which safeguards the growth of the individual. It is what makes liberty and equality effective, for if there is liberty for some but not for all, and equality for a few but not for the majority, what is the remedy? 'The only remedy lies in making fraternity universally effective. What is fraternity? It is nothing but another name for brotherhood of men which is another name for morality. This is why the Buddha preached that Dhamma is morality and as Dhamma is sacred so is morality.'[15]

Book V of *The Buddha and His Dhamma* is entitled 'The Sangh', Book VI 'He and His Contemporaries', Book VII 'The Wanderer's Last Testament', and Book VIII 'The Man who was Siddharth Gautama'. These four books are only half the length of the first four, the last two of them being only half the length of the previous two. From this it would appear that, as the work progressed, Ambedkar became increasingly unsure whether he would live to finish it, and therefore included less and less material in each successive book in order to reach the end of his labours as quickly as possible. But short though the last four books of *The Buddha and His Dhamma* may be their material is as well organized as ever and the points which Ambedkar is concerned to make, whether indirectly through excerpts from the Buddhist scriptures or directly through his own Explanatory Additions, stand out all the more clearly for the succinctness with which he makes them. In Part I of 'The Sangh' Ambedkar gives a brief outline of the organizational structure of the Monastic Order, including a summary of the rules governing admission (he emphasizes that there was no bar of caste, sex, or social status), of the vows taken by the Bhikkhu, and of the procedure to be followed with regard to the trial and punishment of offences. He also has something to say on the subject of 'Confession, called Uposatha', which he describes as 'the most original and unique institution created by the Blessed Lord in connection with the organization of the Bhikkhus'.[16] The Buddha introduced Confession, Ambedkar believes, because he could find no effective way of enforcing certain restrictions which were not offences. 'He therefore thought of Confession in open as a means of organizing [mobilizing?] the Bhikkhu's conscience and making it act as a sentinel to guard him against taking a wrong or false step.'[17] In Part II, 'The Bhikkhu—the Buddha's Conception of Him', Ambedkar outlines, with the help of verses from the Pali *Dhammapada*, the Buddha's conception of what a Bhikkhu should be, answers the question of whether the Bhikkhu is an ascetic, or whether he is the same as the Brahmin, in the negative, and explains the true nature of the distinction between the Bhikkhu and the Upasaka. Part III deals with the Bhikkhu's duty to convert—though not by means of miracles or by force, Part IV with the relations between the Bhikkhu and the laity, and Part V with the Vinaya for the laity, that is, the particular Vinaya or discipline to be observed by the wealthy, by the householder, by children, by a pupil, by husband and wife, by master and servant, and by girls. Book VI, entitled 'He and His Contemporaries', deals with the Buddha's benefactors, with his enemies, with the critics of his doctrines, and with his friends and admirers. Book VII, entitled 'The Wanderer's Last Journey', describes the Buddha's last meetings with those near and dear to him, his departure from Vaishali and arrival in Kushinara, and some of the principal events leading up to his parinirvana or final passing away. Much of the material is taken straight from the Pali *Mahaparinibbana Sutta*, and Ambedkar on the whole allows the text's simple and sublime narrative to speak for itself and make its own impression. When the Buddha has breathed his last his only comment is, 'He was beyond question the light of the world.'[18]

From a practical point of view the most important part of the last four books of *The Buddha and His Dhamma* are perhaps those sections of Book V in which, while doing justice to the historical distinction between the Bhikkhus and the Upasakas or 'lay followers' of the Buddha, Ambedkar at the same time emphasizes the fundamental unity of the Buddhist spiritual community. To him it is obvious that in principle 'the Dhamma was the same for both'.[19] The Bhikkhu and the Upasaka alike observe the Five Precepts, the only difference being (according to Ambedkar) that the Bhikkhu's observance of them is compulsory whereas the Upasaka's is voluntary. Moreover compassion, which is the essence of the Dhamma, requires that everyone shall love and serve, 'and the Bhikkhu is not exempt from it', as some Buddhists thought. Indeed, 'A Bhikkhu who is indifferent to the woes of mankind, however perfect in self-culture, is not at all a Bhikkhu. He may be something else by he is not a Bhikkhu.'[20] Ambedkar also points out that it must not be supposed that, because the Buddha's sermons were addressed to the gathering of the Bhikkhus, what was preached was intended to apply to them only. It applied to both the Bhikkhu and the Upasaka. That the Buddha had the laity in mind when he preached the Five Precepts, the Noble Eightfold Path, and the ten Paramitas or Perfections, 'is quite clear from the very nature of things and no argument, really speaking, is necessary. It is to those who have not left their homes and who are engaged in active life that Panchasila, Ashtanga Marga, and the Paramitas are essential. It is they who are likely to transgress them and not the Bhikkhu who has left home, who is not engaged in active life and who is not likely to transgress them. When the Buddha, therefore, started preaching his Dhamma it must be principally for the laity.'[21] But though the Dhamma was the same for the Bhikkhu and the Upasaka, and though it had been preached more for the benefit of the laity, Ambedkar was very conscious that there was no separate ceremony of Dharma Diksha for those who wanted to be initiated into Buddhism but did not wish to become monks and go forth from home into homelessness. 'This was a very grave omission. It was one of the causes which ultimately led to the downfall of Buddhism in India. For this absence of the initiation ceremony left the laity free to wander from one religion to another and, worse still, follow [two or more religions] at one and the same time.'[22] Probably it was in order to make good this omission, at least to some extent, that Ambedkar included in Book V of *The Buddha and His Dhamma* a separate part dealing with the Vinaya for the laity, thus making it clear that the laity, too, had an ethical and spiritual discipline to observe and that they were not merely the supporters of the monks.

With Book VIII, which is little more than a quarter of the length of Book I, *The Buddha and His Dhamma* ends where it had begun: with the Buddha. Here we are given a thumbnail sketch of 'the Man who was Siddharth Gautama'—as the title of the book significantly styles him—which tells us almost as much about Ambedkar himself as it does about the Buddha. The Buddha's physical appearance was highly pleasing, and the fascination of his personality was such that he exercised an unequalled influence over the hearts and minds of men and women alike. He therefore had the 'capacity to lead', and was respected by his disciples more than the other religious teachers of the day were respected by theirs. Yet his humanity was such that he was full of compassion, a consummate healer of sorrow, concerned for the sick, tolerant of the intolerant, and possessed of a sense of equality and equal treatment, claiming no special privileges for himself. He also had his likes and dislikes. He disliked poverty and the acquisitive instinct, and 'was so fond of the beautiful that he might well bear an *alias* and be called Buddha, the Lover of the Beautiful.'[23]

In his short Epilogue to the work Ambedkar quotes from the tributes which nine modern 'scientists and thinkers', both Indian and Western, have paid to the greatness and uniqueness of the Buddha and his Dhamma, besides reproducing what he calls 'A Vow to Spread His Dhamma' and 'A Prayer for His Return to His Native Land'. The Vow is taken from the Mahayana sutras and is none other than the Bodhisattva's famous fourfold vow, that is, his vow to deliver all beings from suffering, to eradicate all passions, to master all teachings of the Buddha, and to attain Supreme Enlightenment. As for the Prayer, this is taken from the invocation to Amitabha, the Buddha of Infinite Light, with which the great Indian master Vasubandhu opens his commentary on the *Sukhavati-vyuha* or 'Array of the Happy Land' *Sutra*. Patriotically (and perhaps rationalistically) identifying the Happy Land not with Amitabha's Western Pure Land of that name but with India, Ambedkar quotes it in such a way that Vasubandhu's aspiration to attain rebirth there with all his fellow-beings and to proclaim the Truth like Amitabha himself becomes his own heartfelt aspiration to be reborn in his native land and to continue his work for the revival of Buddhism in India.

By appropriating Vasubandhu's invocation in this manner Ambedkar shows his deep feeling for his own country and, what is more, his intense concern for what would happen to the movement of mass conversion after death.

9

After Ambedkar

Bhimrao Ramji Ambedkar died in the early hours of 6 December 1956 and at 7.30 p.m. the following day his body was cremated in Bombay, which had been his headquarters for the greater part of his career and where he still had the greatest number of followers. 500,000 people joined the two mile long funeral procession, which took four hours to make its way from 'Rajagriha', Ambedkar's residence in Dadar, to the local burning ghat, and was the biggest such procession the city had ever seen. Afterwards more than 100,000 of those who had witnessed the cremation escorted the great leader's ashes back to 'Rajagriha'. Before leaving the burning ghat, however, they insisted on fulfilling 'Baba Saheb's' wishes and embracing Buddhism. An impromptu conversion ceremony was accordingly held, and one of the Bhikkhus who was present administered the Three Refuges and Five Precepts to all 100,000 of them on the spot.

From Bombay a portion of the ashes was taken to Delhi where, a week later, a conversion ceremony was held at which 30,000 people were initiated into Buddhism. These same ashes having been divided in their turn and a portion handed over to Ambedkar's followers in Agra a similar ceremony was held in that city too. This time 200,000 people were initiated into

Buddhism. Thus the great movement of mass conversion that had been inaugurated in Nagpur only six weeks earlier continued unabated. Between 7 December 1956 and 10 February 1957 conversion ceremonies were in fact held not only in Bombay, Delhi, and Agra but in more than twenty different towns and cities, most of them within the boundaries of the present day State of Maharashtra, with the result that by the end of that period the number of ex-untouchable Buddhists had risen from 750,000—the number converted by Ambedkar himself in Nagpur and Chanda—to well over 4,000,000.[1] Most of the ceremonies were organized by branches of the Indian Buddhist Society, the body re-founded by Ambedkar in 1955, and the new converts were received into the Buddhist fold either by a leading member of the Republican Party (some of whose office-bearers doubled as office-bearers of the Indian Buddhist Society) or by a Sinhalese or Indian Bhikkhu from the Maha Bodhi Society. Sometimes the new converts would be received into the Buddhist fold by the politician and the Bhikkhu jointly, with the Bhikkhu administering the Three Refuges and Five Precepts and the politician administering the twenty-two vows.

After 10 February 1957, however, the conversion movement was suspended until after the March general elections—the same elections on account of which some of Ambedkar's lieutenants had wanted him to postpone the original mass conversion ceremony. The expectation was that when the elections were over the conversion movement would be not only continued but intensified. This did not, unfortunately, prove to be the case. Though conversion ceremonies indeed continued to be held all over central and western India, and even farther afield, with the exception of that held at Aligarh on 13 April, when 200,000 people embraced Buddhism, they were on the whole smaller and less spectacular affairs than before. This may have been due to the fact that the conversion movement, having been virtually suspended for two crucial months, had now lost much of its original impetus and that what had been lost could not easily be regained. It may equally have been due to the fact that the movement had reached what were, for the time being, its natural limits. Though Ambedkar was held in the highest esteem by all the untouchable communities of India his influence was greatest within his own Mahar community, and it was the Mahars who had responded most enthusiastically to his call to embrace Buddhism. Once the Mahars had been converted, therefore, the conversion movement naturally slowed down, the more especially since Ambedkar himself was no longer present to convince the other untouchable communities of the rightness of the step he had taken and persuade them to do likewise.

The fact that the conversion movement had reached its natural limits by the beginning of 1957 was reflected in the official statistics. According to the 1961 census returns there were 3,250,227 Buddhists in India (an increase of 1,671 per cent over the 1951 figure), of whom 2,789,501 were to be found in Maharashtra as compared with 2,489 ten years earlier. The increase in the number of Buddhists in Maharashtra was thus out of all proportion to the increase in the rest of the country. By 1971, however, the figures had risen only very slightly and there were altogether 3,812,325 registered Buddhists in India, from which fact it was clear that even though a number of conversion ceremonies had been held outside Maharashtra the movement of mass conversion among the Mahars had not been followed by any corresponding movement among the other untouchable communities.

Not that the statistics in question were completely accurate. The newly converted Buddhists themselves were convinced that they were very inaccurate indeed and that the number of Buddhists in India was actually far greater than the census returns showed, and in this they were undoubtedly right, though perhaps not quite to the extent that some of them believed. (According to one source, by March 1959 'nearly 15 to 20 million Untouchables had embraced Buddhism'.)[2] There were two reasons for the discrepancy between the official figures, on the one hand, and the facts as known to the Buddhists themselves on the other. In the first place the census-takers, most of whom were Caste Hindus, in some cases deliberately enumerated Buddhists as Hindus in order to minimize the extent, and therefore the significance, of the conversion movement. (In 1951, at the time of the first post-independence census, I had myself been enumerated, despite my vigorous protests, as 'Hindu by religion and Buddhist by caste'.) In the second place, many of those who had embraced Buddhism at one or another of the conversion ceremonies, and who therefore appeared in the Buddhists' own statistics, did not officially declare themselves as Buddhists, and hence were not included as such in the census returns. Some of those who thus remained suspended in a kind of limbo, able neither really to leave the hell of Hinduism and caste nor really to enter the heaven of Buddhism and equality, were unwilling to declare themselves Buddhists because they were afraid that, if they did so, they would be subject to harassment by the more militant Caste Hindus, who in some places were actually attacking and killing the newly converted Buddhists for daring to renounce their ancestral religion. Others, and these were the more numerous, were unwilling to declare themselves as Buddhists because they did not want to forgo the scholarships and stipends and other benefits to which they were entitled as members of the Scheduled Castes and which, they believed, were essential to their advancement.

These social and educational 'concessions', as they were significantly termed, were given by the Central Government and by the various State Governments, and they were given not on account of the recipient's religion but solely because of the extreme poverty, as well as the social and educational backwardness, of the community to which he happened to belong. Nonetheless, a few weeks after the general elections both the Central Government and the State Government of Bombay, of which Maharashtra was then a part and in which the majority of newly converted Buddhists were to be found, stopped giving scholarships and stipends to those students who had declared themselves Buddhists, or whose parents had declared themselves Buddhists, even though change of religion had not made the slightest difference to their economic position. Despite appeals from the Maha Bodhi Society and other Buddhist organizations, as well as from various humanitarian groups, the Government of India refused to rescind its decision, ostensibly on constitutional grounds, so that the ex-untouchable Buddhist students lost their Central scholarships and stipends for good. The State Government of Bombay fortunately adopted a more generous and far-sighted policy and, early in 1958, restored to the untouchable Buddhist students the scholarships and stipends which formerly they had enjoyed as members of the Scheduled Castes. Thus a situation was created in which ex-untouchable Buddhist students were not entitled to their former Central Government concessions anywhere in India, including the State of Bombay, and in which they were entitled to the corresponding State Government concessions only in the State of Bombay. This meant that the ex-untouchable Buddhist students in the State of Bombay had a decided advantage over their opposite numbers in other States and that they—and their parents—had, therefore, less inducement *not* to declare themselves as Buddhists.

Some twenty years later, ex-untouchable Buddhist observers in other parts of the country were inclined to attribute the greater success of the conversion movement in Maharashtra to the fact that there members of the Scheduled Castes could declare themselves Buddhists without having to forgo their State as well as their Central Government concessions, thus enjoying, if only to a limited extent, the best of both worlds. Such observers were, however, mistaken. While the concessions undoubtedly helped, the real reason for the greater success of the conversion movement in Maharashtra was to be found in the courage and determination of the former Mahars, in their readiness to make sacrifices, and, above all, in their unswerving loyalty to the memory of their great leader and emancipator.

But though ex-untouchable Buddhists in the State of Bombay/Maharashtra had less inducement not to declare themselves Buddhists than did their opposite numbers elsewhere in India, this did not mean that they had no such inducement at all. The social and educational concessions given by the Central Government were often of greater monetary value than those given by the State Government, and students from very poor families were sometimes tempted to apply for the former rather than for the latter even after taking the Dharma Diksha and becoming (unofficial) Buddhists. Though cases of this sort were not common, there were enough of them to give rise to serious differences of opinion not only among the students themselves but also among their elders and, indeed, within large sections of the Mahar-cum-Buddhist community. Some people thought that all true followers of 'Baba Saheb' should take Dharma Diksha at the first opportunity and declare themselves Buddhists regardless of consequences and that this applied to students as much as to anybody else. Others thought that it was—or that it was not—dishonest and, in effect, even a breach of the fourth precept (the precept to abstain from false speech), to apply for Central Government concessions after taking Dharma Diksha, while yet others thought that even if it was a breach of the fourth precept such a breach was—or was not—justified in the circumstances. Others, again, simply did not know what to think. Thus the subject of Central Government concessions was the source of a good deal of confusion and since this confusion was never really cleared up it gave rise to a feeling of uncertainty which, in its turn, tended to have an undermining effect on the conversion movement.

The vexed subject of Central Government concessions was not, however, the only source of confusion among Ambedkar's followers, or even the most serious. For many years the most serious source of confusion was, perhaps, the fact that having renounced Hinduism the newly converted Buddhists—most of whom were both poor and illiterate—had little or no means of finding out what Buddhism really meant or how they were supposed to practise it and, for this reason, often continued to keep up un-Buddhistic customs and observances which they had in theory repudiated. In this they were hardly to blame. What usually happened was that they turned up at a mass conversion ceremony, were received into the Buddhist fold by a visiting politician or Maha Bodhi Society Bhikkhu, donated some money, and then went back to their ghettoes in city, town, or village to work (if they could get work), to support their families and, in some cases, to suffer harrassment at the hands of their Caste Hindu neighbours. The politician they probably did not see again until the time of the next election, while the Maha Bodhi Society Bhikkhu they probably did not see again at all. In other words there was no follow up and in virtually all cases those who had taken the Dharma Diksha had no one to teach them anything about Buddhism. The politicians who conducted the conversion ceremonies were not in a position to teach them because with very few exceptions they knew little or nothing about the Dharma themselves and because they were, in any case, too busy campaigning for votes, collecting funds, and (after a few years) fighting among themselves to have much time for anything else. (Some of them indeed added to the existing confusion by denying that they were Buddhists in order to be able to contest seats reserved for members of the Scheduled Castes who were, of course, by definition Hindu.) As for the Maha Bodhi Society Bhikkhus, of whom there were less than a dozen stationed in Bombay, Delhi, Sanchi, Lucknow, and Sarnath, though these had a scholarly knowledge of the Dharma they were too busy running the Society's centres and looking after foreign Buddhist pilgrims to be able to do much more than conduct conversion ceremonies and deliver the occasional lecture.

Ambedkar had, of course, hoped that help in teaching his followers would be forthcoming from the rest of the Buddhist world and a handful of Bhikkhus from south-east Asia did, in fact, find their way to the tiny makeshift temples that soon were springing up all over central and western India, wherever there were more than a few hundred newly converted Buddhists. But as Ambedkar had also feared, the Bhikkhus proved to be not very adaptable and for one reason or another did not stay very long or achieve very much. Besides having trouble with the local language (or languages), they found it difficult to adjust to a standard of living so much lower than that to which they were accustomed and difficult to relate to Buddhists who, devoted as they obviously were, failed to treat them with the extreme formal deference with which they were invariably treated in their own country. They also found it difficult to understand the social, economic, and religious background of the newly converted Buddhists and still more difficult to appreciate the depth of their loyalty to Ambedkar and the extent to which the great leader's memory dominated their thinking. Above all, they found it difficult to teach the Dharma—difficult, that is, to teach it in such a way that their hearers could grasp its basic principles and apply them to their own lives. This was due partly to the fact that newly converted Buddhists did not always share their mentors' assumptions and partly to the fact that the Bhikkhus themselves were more familiar with the letter of the Dharma than with its spirit and could present it only in the stereotype form in which it had been handed down to them. Thus the newly converted Buddhists did not learn very much and only too often were left feeling that they had, in biblical phrase, asked for bread and been given a stone. When the Bhikkhus realized that their efforts on behalf of the Dharma were not meeting with the success they had expected they attributed it to their hearers' lack of faith and told them that, if they really wanted to understand Buddhism, they would have to go to Ceylon or Thailand (as the case might be), become monks, and spend several years studying Pali.

Not unnaturally, the vast majority of the newly converted Buddhists had no wish to go to Ceylon or Thailand, or to become monks, or even to spend several years studying Pali. They did, however, very much want to know more about Buddhism and if anyone took the trouble to explain it to them in a way that they could understand their joy, enthusiasm, and gratitude knew no bounds. Certainly this was my own experience when, as a result of the link that I had forged with them in Nagpur during the anxious days immediately following Ambedkar's death, I undertook a series of four preaching tours that lasted, with very little intermission, from February 1959 to May 1961. In the course of these tours I visited cities, towns, and villages in more than half the states of India, opened temples and libraries, installed images of the Buddha, performed name-giving ceremonies and after-death ceremonies, blessed marriages, conferred with leading members of the Indian Buddhist Society, held a special training course, delivered about 400 lectures and personally initiated upwards of 100,000 people into Buddhism. With each succeeding tour, however, my activities came to be increasingly concentrated in and around Nagpur, Bombay, Poona, Jabalpur, and Ahmedabad, but especially in and around Poona, where I eventually established a sort of seasonal headquarters. The reason for this was that in Poona I had the co-operation of a group of idealistic young men, mostly college students, who for more than a year before my arrival had been publicly reading and explaining *The Buddha and His Dhamma* every Sunday morning for the benefit of their less literate fellow Buddhists. Moreover, Poona was not only the centre of Maharashtrian culture but the citadel of Brahminical orthodoxy, so that if it was possible to establish Buddhism in Poona it was possible to establish it anywhere in Maharashtra.

In 1963, two years after I had returned to Kalimpong from the fourth and longest of my preaching tours, I was invited by the English Sangha Trust to take charge of their Vihara in north-west London. By this time the fighting between the politicians had led to a series of splits in the Republican Party and these had resulted in serious divisions among the newly converted Buddhists, even so far as religious activities were concerned. Partly for this reason, and partly because I had now spent twenty years in the East, I eventually accepted the Trust's invitation and accordingly left India for the United Kingdom in August 1964. Though I had originally agreed to take charge of the Hampstead Buddhist Vihara for six months, I ended up staying there for more than two years. During this period I came to the conclusion that conditions in Britain were favourable to the spread of the Dharma and therefore decided to transfer my permanent headquarters from Kalimpong to London. Before actually doing so, however, I returned to India for a three-month preaching tour that culminated in Nagpur where, on the tenth anniversary of Ambedkar's death, I addressed a gathering of 100,000 people. In the course of the tour I explained to my friends and disciples what I was doing and bade them farewell. In future, I told them, I would be dividing my time between England, the country of my birth, and India, the country of my adoption, and hoped to spend six months in each of them alternately.

This hope was not to be fulfilled. Shortly after my final departure from India it had been borne in upon me that if full advantage was to be taken of the fact that conditions in Britain were favourable to the spread of Buddhism there would have to be a new Buddhist movement there, and since the creation of this new Buddhist movement took longer than I had expected it was twelve years before I saw India again. In the meantime, however, I kept in touch with my old friends and disciples among the 'newly converted' Buddhists in Poona and elsewhere and in 1977 one of my senior English disciples paid them a fraternal visit which eventually led to the creation of a new Buddhist movement in India too. As a result of this development, between February 1979 and December 1983 I paid four visits to India and on each occasion delivered lectures and performed ceremonies in the same way as before and, in some cases, for the benefit of the very same people.

The longest and perhaps most important of these visits took place in the winter of 1981—82, when I went on a preaching tour that took me to Bombay, Delhi, Ahmedabad, and Ajmer, as well as to Poona and about fifty other towns and villages of Marathwada, as the six districts that constitute the heart of Maharashtra were collectively termed. In the course of this visit, in particular, I was able to see for myself what sort of changes had taken place among Ambedkar's followers and whether the conversion movement had made any progress. There was little doubt that as a community they were marginally more prosperous than before (few of the people attending my lectures were now dressed in rags), though perhaps it would be more correct to say that they were marginally less poverty-stricken. Quite a few of the more well off among them owned motor scooters, while one or two who had risen to gazetted officer rank in Central Government service had small cars and, of course, chauffeurs. It was evident, however, that whatever meagre wealth had accrued to Ambedkar's followers was very unevenly distributed, and that the vast majority of them lived well below even the Indian poverty line. It was also evident that there had been very little change in the attitude of the Caste Hindus towards them. Reports of atrocities committed on 'Harijans' continued to appear with nauseating regularity in the national press, yet though the offenders were sometimes caught and punished the conscience of Caste Hindu India on the whole remained untouched.

So far as the conversion movement itself was concerned, not much had really happened. As before, it was confined mainly to

171

Maharashtra and to the ex-Mahars, and as before the principal reason for the lack of progress was the fact that those who had taken Dharma Diksha had no one to teach them anything about Buddhism. In some areas they had not had an opportunity of hearing a real lecture on Buddhism since my own preaching tours of a generation ago, while in others they had never had such an opportunity, and in a community where so many were illiterate and, therefore, entirely dependent for their knowledge of Buddhism on the spoken word, this was a serious deprivation. Yet even though they had not had anyone to teach them, the vast majority of those who had embraced Buddhism in response to Ambedkar's call had lost neither their faith in their great leader's vision nor their desire to learn more about the religion to which he had directed them. The evidences of that faith and that desire were to be found all over Maharashtra, and even beyond. Wherever I went, in the course of that preaching tour in the winter of 1981—82, I saw not only scores of newly constructed Buddhist temples but hundreds of lifesize—and more than lifesize—busts and statues of Ambedkar. Cast in bronze, or merely moulded in plaster, the familiar figure was to be seen in every town and village, in death as in life dominating the lives of his people and reminding the whole nation of the principles for which he had stood.

Wherever I went I moreover saw, as I had seen time and time again all those years ago, how overwhelmingly grateful Ambedkar's followers were for whatever Buddhist teaching they received. This time, however, they would not have to wait for years before they heard another lecture on Buddhism. This time they were in contact with a new Buddhist movement, a movement that was the direct continuation of Ambedkar's own work for the Dharma, so that even after I had gone there would be plenty of opportunities for them to hear lectures, to learn how to meditate, and to go on retreat. There would, in short, be plenty of opportunities for them to practise Buddhism, and it was in the individual and collective practise of Buddhism that— Ambedkar believed—they would find the inspiration which would enable them, after centuries of oppression, to transform every aspect of their lives.

Notes

1. The Significance of Ambedkar

1 This was Ambedkar's own figure, as given in his letter to Devapriya Valisinha dated 30 October 1956. *The Maha Bodhi* (Calcutta), Vol. 65, p. 226

3. The Hell of Caste

1 B. R. Ambedkar, *Annihilation of Caste* (Jalandhar, n. d.) p. 83. Also Dr Babasaheb Ambedkar, *Writings and Speeches* Vol. 1 (Bombay 1979), p. 52
2 Quoted in Dhananjay Keer, *Mahatma Jotirao Phooley: Father of the Indian Social Revolution* (Bombay 1964. Second edition 1974), p. 115
3 B. R. Ambedkar, *The Untouchables* (Third edition, Balrampur 1977), p. 27
4 Quoted in B. R. Ambedkar, *Who Were the Shudras?* (Bombay 1946. Reprinted 1970), pp. 38—39
5 *Annihilation of Caste*, p. 93. Also *Writings and Speeches* Vol. 1, p. 57

6 *The Untouchables,* p. 26
7 7*Mahatma Jotirao Phooley: Father of the Indian Social Revolution,* p. 41
8 Bhagwan Das (ed.), *Thus Spoke Ambedkar* Vol. 4 (Bangalore n. d.), pp. 67—68
9 *Ibid.,* pp. 68—69

4. Milestones on the Road to Conversion

1 B. G. Kunte (Compiler), *Source Material on Dr Baba Saheb Ambedkar and the Movement of Untouchables* Vol. 1 (Bombay 1982), p. 485
2 *Ibid.,* p. 487
3 *Ibid.,* p. 487
4 Dhananjay Keer, *Dr Ambedkar: Life and Mission* (Second edition, Bombay 1962), p. 106
5 *Ibid.,* p. 170
6 Maha Sthavira Sangharakshita, *The Ten Pillars of Buddhism* (Second edition London 1984), p. 27
7 Keer, p. 254
8 Bhagwan Das (ed.), *Thus Spoke Ambedkar* Vol. 4 (Bangalore n. d.), p. 257
9 *Ibid.,* p. 110
10 *Ibid.,* p. 111
11 *Ibid.,* pp. 112—113
12 *Ibid.,* p. 113
13 *Ibid.,* p. 111
14 *Ibid.,* pp. 71—72
15 *Ibid.,* pp. 64—65. The source of Ambedkar's quotation is Digha Nikaya xvi. 2. 25—26. Tr. T. W. and C. A. F. Rhys Davids, *Dialogues of the Buddha* Part II (Fourth edition, London 1959), pp. 107—108. In rendering the Buddha's words into Marathi Ambedkar paraphrased them slightly
16 Bhagwan Das (Selected and edited), *Rare Prefaces Written by Dr Baba Saheb B. R. Ambedkar* (Jullundur 1980), p. 20
17 D. C. Ahir (ed.), *Dr Ambedkar on Buddhism* (Bombay 1982), p. 97

18 Kunte, p. 366
19 *Ibid.*, p. 368
20 B. R. Ambedkar, *Buddha and the Future of His Religion* (Jullundur 1980), p. 12
21 Bhagwan Das (ed.), *Thus Spoke Ambedkar* Vol. 2 (Jullundur n. d.), pp. 124—125. Kunte, pp. 371—372
22 Kunte, p. 274
23 Ahir, pp. 14—15
24 *Ibid.*, p. 73
25 Kunte, p. 406
26 Keer, p. 456
27 Ahir, p. 17
28 *Ibid.*, p. 55
29 Keer, p. 493

5. The Search for Roots

1 B. G. Kunte (Compiler), *Source Material on Dr Babasaheb Ambedkar and the Movement of Untouchables* vol. 1 (Bombay 1982), p. 171
2 *Ibid.*, p. 212
3 B. R. Ambedkar, *Who Were the Shudras?* (Bombay 1946. Reprinted 1970), p. xi
4 *Ibid.*, p. xv
5 Curiously enough, in the Hindu law books a Shudra is termed a graveyard
6 B. R. Ambedkar, *The Untouchables* (Third edition, Balrampur 1977), p. xvi
7 *Ibid.*, p. xvii
8 *Ibid.*, pp. 43—44
9 *Ibid.*, p. 101
10 *Ibid.*, p. 105
11 *Ibid.*, p. 153
12 *Ibid.*, p. 168
13 *Ibid.*, p. 204

6. Thinking About Buddhism

1 B. R. Ambedkar, *Buddha and the Future of His Religion* (Third edition, Jullundur 1980), p. 3
2 *Ibid.*, pp. 3—4
3 *Ibid.*, p. 4
4 *Ibid.*, p. 4
5 T. W. and C. A. F. Rhys Davids, *Dialogues of the Buddha* Part II (Fourth edition, London 1959), p. 171
6 T. W. Rhys Davids, *The Questions of King Milinda* (The Sacred Books of the East Vol XXXV. Oxford 1890), p. 202
7 *Buddha and the Future of His Religion*, p. 4
8 *Ibid.*, p. 4
9 *Ibid.*, p. 5
10 *Ibid.*, p. 5
11 *Ibid.*, p. 5
12 *Ibid.*, pp. 5—6
13 *Ibid.*, p. 6
14 *Ibid.*, p. 7
15 *Ibid.*, p. 7
16 Dr Baba Saheb Ambedkar, *Writings and Speeches* Vol. 1 (Bombay 1979), p. 58
17 *Buddha and the Future of His Religion*, p. 6
18 *Ibid.*, p. 7
19 *Ibid.*, p. 8
20 *Ibid.*, p. 10
21 *Ibid.*, p. 11
22 *Ibid.*, p. 11
23 *Ibid.*, p. 11
24 *Ibid.*, p. 12
25 *Ibid.*, p. 12
26 *Ibid.*, p. 12
27 Dr Baba Saheb Ambedkar, *Writings and Speeches* Vol. 1 (Bombay 1979), p. 57
28 *Ibid.*, p. 57
29 *Buddha and the Future of His Religion*, p. 12
30 *Ibid.*, p. 12
31 *Ibid.*, p. 12

32 *Ibid.*, p. 13
33 *Ibid.*, p. 13
34 *Ibid.*, p. 13
35 *Ibid.*, p. 13
36 *Ibid.*, p. 13
37 *Ibid.*, p. 14
38 *Ibid.*, p. 14
39 *Ibid.*, p. 14
40 *Ibid.*, p. 14
41 *Ibid.*, p. 14
42 *Ibid.*, p. 15
43 *Ibid.*, p. 15
44 *Ibid.*, p. 15
45 *Ibid.*, p. 15
46 *Ibid.*, p. 15
47 *Ibid.*, p. 15
48 James Hastings (ed.), *Encyclopaedia of Religion and Ethics* Vol. 7 (Edinburgh 1914), p. 501b
49 *Ibid.*, p. 502a
50 *Buddha and the Future of His Religion,* pp. 15—16
51 *Ibid.*, p. 16
52 *Ibid.*, p. 16
53 *Ibid.*, p. 16
54 *Ibid.*, p. 16
55 *Ibid.*, p. 16

7. The Great Mass Conversion

1 Bhagwan Das (ed.), *Thus Spoke Ambedkar* vol. 2 (Jullundur n. d.), pp. 141—142
2 Dhananjay Keer, *Dr Ambedkar: Life and Mission* (Second edition, Bombay 1962), p. 495
3 Keer, p. 495
4 Bhagwan Das (ed.), *Thus Spoke Ambedkar* (Bangalore n. d.), pp. 272—274
5 Keer, p. 501
6 *Thus Spoke Ambedkar,* vol. 2, p. 147

7 *Ibid.*, p. 148
8 *Ibid.*, p. 150

8. The Buddha and His Dhamma

1 Bhagwan Das (ed.), *Rare Prefaces Written by Dr Ambedkar* (Jullundur 1980), pp. 28—29
2 *Ibid.*, p. 29
3 Dhananjay Keer, *Dr Ambedkar: Life and Mission* (Second edition, Bombay 1962), p. 488
4 B. R. Ambedkar, *Buddha and the Future of His Religion* (Third edition, Jullundur 1980), p. 14
5 B. R. Ambedkar, *The Buddha and His Dhamma* (Second edition, Bombay 1974), p. 80
6 *Ibid.*, p. 80
7 *Ibid.*, p. xlii
8 *Ibid.*, p. 91
9 *Ibid.*, p. 80
10 *Ibid.*, p. 159
11 *Ibid.*, p. 232
12 *Ibid.*, p. 231
13 *Ibid.*, p. 231
14 *Ibid.*, p. 231
15 *Ibid.*, p. 234
16 *Ibid.*, p. 309
17 *Ibid.*, p. 310
18 *Ibid.*, p. 401
19 *Ibid.*, p. 331
20 *Ibid.*, p. 319
21 *Ibid.*, p. 330
22 *Ibid.*, p. 328
23 *Ibid.*, p. 425

9. After Ambedkar

1 Shri Sankarananda Shastri, 'A Report on the Conversion

Movement'. *The Maha Bodhi* (Calcutta), vol. 65, pp. 128—130
2 S. N. Shastri, M.A., M.O.L., 'Revival of Buddism in India'.
The Maha Bodhi (Calcutta), vol. 67, p. 67

Further Reading

Ambedkar, B. R.	*Annihilation of Caste* (Bheem Patrika, Jullundur)
,,	*The Buddha and His Dhamma* (Siddharth, Bombay)
,,	*The Untouchables* (Jetavana Mahavihara, Shravasti)
,,	*What Congress and Gandhi Have Done to the Untouchables* (Thacker & Co., Bombay)
Ahir, D. C.	*Dr Ambedkar On Buddhism* (Siddharth, Bombay)
Das, Bhagwan	*Thus Spoke Ambedkar* (Volumes 1—4) (Ambedkar Sahithya Prakashana, Bangalore)
Hiro, Dilip	*The Untouchables of India* (Report no. 26 (1982) of the Minority Rights Group, London)
Jatava, D. R.	*The Social Philosophy of Dr B. R. Ambedkar* (Phoenix Publishing Agency, Agra)
,,	*The Political Philosophy of Dr B. R. Ambedkar* (Phoenix Publishing Agency, Agra)
Joshi, B. R.	*Untouchable! Voices of the Dalit Liberation Movement* (The Minority Rights Group, London)

Keer, Dhananjay	*Dr Ambedkar: Life and Mission* (Popular Prakashan, Bombay)
,,	*Mahatma Jotirao Phooley: Father of the Indian Social Revolution* (Popular Prakashan, Bombay)
Ling, Trevor	*Buddhist Revival in India: Aspects of the Sociology of Buddhism* (Macmillan, London)
Lokhande, G. S.	*Bhimrao Ramji Ambedkar: A Study in Social Democracy* (Intellectual Publishing House, New Delhi)
Zelliot, Eleanor	*Gandhi and Ambedkar: A Study in Leadership* (Triratna Grantha Mala, Poona)

All of the above titles can be ordered through the Bookshop at *The London Buddhist Centre, 51 Roman Road, London E2 0HU*

Also from Windhorse Publications

JAI BHIM!
Dispatches from a Peaceful Revolution
By Terry Pilchick

This book is in many ways a sequel to *Ambedkar and Buddhism*. In 1978, a number of Sangharakshita's Western disciples went out to India to establish a new Buddhist movement especially tailored to the needs of Dr. Ambedkar's modern followers. *Jai Bhim! Dispatches from a Peaceful Revolution* explains what has happened as a result.

In 1982 and 1985, Terry Pilchick made two extended visits to India. Travelling around the Buddhist localities with Sangharakshita, he was able to witness a unique experiment in social change based on non-violence, personal growth, and mutual co-operation. This book is at once a record of what he saw, and a moving tribute to Dr Ambedkar's mass conversion movement.

Rich in bizarre detail and peopled by a cast of warmly sketched characters, this first-hand account offers a powerful argument for the effectiveness of grassroots social action which should be read by anyone interested in achieving a fairer world without violence.

240 pages
Paperback. Price £5.95
ISBN 0 904766 36 5